PRACTICALLY USELESS INFORMATION™

Weddings

**Also in the
PRACTICALLY USELESS INFORMATION™
Series:**

❧

Food & Drink

PRACTICALLY USELESS INFORMATION™

Weddings

A Kolpas Compendium™

Norman Kolpas
Katie Kolpas

RUTLEDGE HILL PRESS
Nashville, Tennessee
A Division of Thomas Nelson Publishers
Since 1798

www.thomasnelson.com

Published by Rutledge Hill Press, a Division of Thomas Nelson, Inc., P.O. Box 141000, Nashville, Tennessee 37214.

Rutledge Hill books may be purchased in bulk for educational, business, fundraising, or sales promotional use. For information, please e-mail SpecialMarkets@ThomasNelson.com.

Design by Gore Studio Inc.

Library of Congress Cataloging-in-Publication Data

Kolpas, Norman.
　　Practically useless information. Weddings/Norman Kolpas, Katie Kolpas.
　　　　p. cm.—(Practically useless information)
　　Includes bibliographical references and index.
　　ISBN 1-4016-0206-1 (hardcover)
　　1. Weddings—Miscellanea. 2. Marriage—Miscellanea. I. Title: Weddings.
II. Kolpas, Katie, 1960– III. Title. IV. Series.

　　GT2690.K66 2005
　　395.2'2—dc22

2004022900

Printed in the United States of America

05 06 07 08 09—5 4 3 2 1

FOR JAKE

❤

"The value of marriage is not that adults
produce children but that children produce adults."
—*Tunnel of Love* (1958), Peter De Vries

Some Acknowledgments

♥♥

We would both like to thank everyone at Rutledge Hill Press and Thomas Nelson for their enthusiastic support of this book. Special mention goes to Larry Stone and Bryan Curtis, who immediately understood the book's appeal; and to David Dunham, who first introduced us to all the wonderful people at Thomas Nelson, including Pamela Clements, Rutledge Hill's new associate publisher. Jennifer Greenstein was a refreshingly calm and steady editor. And Tracey Menges and Tina Goodrow deserve thanks for keeping everything moving smoothly and with old-fashioned Southern charm. Thanks also to copy editor Sara Henry for her keen eye, to designer Bruce Gore for his classic treatment of the material, and to typesetter Lindsay Carreker for her painstaking good work.

Norman would also like to thank Katie: You've been such a complete and total partner and supporter from the day I met you, and you prove continually that, even though we're sometimes a tired old married couple, we can still dedicate ourselves to fun.

Katie would also like to thank Norman: Though I'd dreamed of being married since I was a girl, I never imagined how wonderful marriage could be.

Introduction

♥♥

Welcome to the one book on weddings and marriage you need the most: a book that offers virtually no practical information at all.

Please let us explain.

If you're engaged to be married, chances are you've already started making wedding plans. Statistics show there is a strong likelihood that you've hired or are thinking about hiring a wedding planner or consultant. At the very least, you've already cruised the many wedding Web sites on the Internet, and you've probably bought or have been given one or more books that promise to take you step by step through the whole process of throwing a wedding.

And that doesn't even begin to touch on the advice and help—real or meddlesome—you've begun to receive from family and friends.

In short, with your wedding months, weeks, or days away, you've begun to feel as if you're rapidly going nuts. That is why this particular book is so important.

You need a diversion. You need some fun. You need someone or something that restores your sanity, or reflects your insanity, or at least sets your world in slightly better balance.

After all the supposedly helpful information you're being constantly bombarded with, you desperately need some truly *useless* information.

The following pages are packed with precisely that.

We know what it's like. Though we got married way back in 1987, the memories of our five-month-and-one-week-long engagement (eight months and three weeks shorter than the national average) remain as fresh as if they happened yesterday:

- ➤ We searched for the perfect venue (rejecting The Screaming Clam disco in Malibu and settling contentedly on Katie's mother's and stepfather's house).
- ➤ We searched for the perfect invitation (which we wrote ourselves, using very traditional language, and then convinced our printer, a friend of the family, to set in classic, non-flowery, Times Roman font on sturdy cream-colored stock).
- ➤ We searched for the perfect music (finally hiring a trio of middle-aged

jazz cats who looked like they didn't know the meaning of sunshine or fresh fruits and vegetables).

- We (or, rather, Katie and her mom, Susan) searched for the perfect wedding dress (and on the very first try of the very first day, they found one that fit her perfectly, made from antique lace, in the window of the shop owned by the same dressmaker who created the wedding gown Meryl Streep wore in the movie based on Nora Ephron's novel *Heartburn*).
- We (or, rather, Norman, with Katie offering tactful advice) searched for the perfect wedding suit (and Norman finally bought it off the rack at Nordstrom).
- We searched for the perfect officiant (and a friend of a friend introduced us to Rabbi Scott, who led an informal congregation of young performing artists and had just the right relaxed-yet-traditional, down-to-earth spirit we had hoped for).

The entire process felt like one long search. And the one thing we really felt like we needed all along was a break from all our searching.

That welcome break is now in your hands.

If you're searching for important facts, pointers, guidelines, and checklists for your wedding, keep looking.

But if you want information that is interesting, romantic, offbeat, or oddball on the topic of weddings and marriage, flip to any page in this book and you will find it, several times over.

Oh, how we wish we'd had a book like this back in late 1986 and early 1987! Instead of fretting over the latest little detail gone awry, we could have amused or diverted each other with such need-to-know stuff as

- The best weather months for weddings in Bangkok, Tripoli, Baghdad, Karachi, or Managua (pages 90–93)
- Pennsylvania founder William Penn's advice for a good marriage (page 94)
- Some Italian or Greek wedding customs (pages 21 and 68)
- Assorted strange laws related to courtship, weddings, and marriage (pages 16, 82, 125, and 166)
- Some eerily prophetic fortune-cookie fortunes (pages 118–119)

Any of those bits of information would have been the perfect antidote to the more practical wedding-related thoughts that were usually swirling in our heads.

Of course, you've probably noticed that the title of this book includes a form of the word "practical" in its title. There's a good reason.

This book actually had its start as the two of us faced our 16th wedding anniversary. "Are there any traditional gifts for a 16th anniversary?" we wondered. We looked for an answer and wound up compiling a comprehensive chart detailing anniversary gifts, both traditional and modern, all the way up to the 100th anniversary (pages 168–169). Then, we found ourselves wishing for the sort of wacky book that would include such a chart, along with other information that many people, depending on their circumstances, might dismiss as useless—but that we found fascinating.

Most of the seemingly useless information in this book might actually be practical to you, or to someone, at some time or other. You might actually be planning to get married in Karachi. Or maybe some of those fortunes could become sayings you use in special fortune cookies you hand out as favors to your wedding guests.

You might find inspiration in some of the wedding customs or prayers of different nations, peoples, or faiths scattered throughout these pages. Perhaps a random quote scattered here or there, a classic verse, or a literary passage might inspire, or become part of, your own wedding vows.

Or you, like the two of us, might just be an old married couple who still finds the whole topic of weddings fascinating, fun, and inspiring. (Yes, it *can* come to feel that way after the craziness of the event has passed.) In that case, the entire book itself can feel uncannily practical.

However you use this book, we hope you'll have as much fun with it as we had putting it together.

SIX BASIC WEDDING GOWN SHAPES

▼▼

A-line: Close-fitting bodice and waist with A-shaped skirt to the floor. A classic, flattering to most body types.

Ball gown: Full bodice and gathered waist, with very full skirt. A fairy tale look good for all shapes.

Empire: Full, nicely fitted bodice and high waist, with a flowing but narrow A-shaped skirt beneath. Flattering for all shapes.

Mermaid: Form-fitting gown that flairs out below the knee to the floor. Flattering for a curvy figure.

Princess: See *A-Line*.

Sheath: Form-fitting full-length dress for slender, tall, or petite brides.

MELLOW BELLS

▼▼

Hear the mellow wedding bells,
Golden bells!
What a world of happiness their harmony foretells!
Through the balmy air of night
How they ring out their delight!
From the molten-golden notes,
And all in tune,
What a liquid ditty floats
To the turtle-dove that listens, while she gloats
On the moon!
Oh, from out the sounding cells,
What a gush of euphony voluminously wells!
How it swells!
How it dwells
On the Future! how it tells
Of the rapture that impels
To the swinging and the ringing
Of the bells, bells, bells,
Of the bells, bells, bells, bells,
Bells, bells, bells -
To the rhyming and the chiming of the bells!
—"The Bells" (1849), Edgar Allan Poe

DINNER MENU FOR A SPANISH ROYAL WEDDING

❤❤

The following menu, devised by Juan Maria Arzak and Ferrán Adriá with the help of Francisco Roncero, was served at the matrimonial banquet following the May 22, 2004, wedding of His Royal Highness Felipe, Crown Prince of Asturias, and Miss Letizia Ortiz Rocasolano—the first Spanish royal wedding held in almost a century.

Aperitivos variados
[Varied appetizers]
❦

Yemas de Espárragos blancos de Tudela con trufa de verano y su sopa
[Asparaus Tips from Tudela with Summer Truffle and Its Soup]
❦

Rape con habitas a la menta, ravioli ibérico de tomato y vinagre de Jérez
[Skate with Broad Beans, Tomato, Ravioli, and Sherry Vinegar]
❦

Pechuga de pato en escabeche ligero al vino tinto, puré de limón
[Lightly Marinated Duck Breast in Red Wine with Lemon Puree]
❦

Postre: Chocolate, coco, frutos rojos con sorbete de cítricos
[Dessert: Chocolate, coconut, assorted red fruits, with citrus sorbet]
❦

Vinos [Wines]:
Clarión Viñas del Vero (Somontano Aragón)
Milmanda Torres (Cuenca la Barberá) Blanco
Chivite colección 125 (D.O. Navarra) Blanco
Matarromera (Ribera del Duero) Tinto
M.R. Moscatel (D.O. Málaga)

THE HERB OF LOVE

❤❤

The wonderfully fragrant herb rosemary, long associated with Aphrodite, the Greek goddess of love, has for centuries been included in marriage celebrations. In Tudor England, it decorated churches and banqueting halls for weddings, and sprigs of the herb even scented the wine goblets with which guests toasted the bride and groom.

THE FOUR C'S (AND ONE P) OF DIAMONDS

▼▼▼

The quality of all diamonds is judged on the basis of four classic criteria, each of which begins with the letter "C." In addition, famed jeweler Tiffany & Co. has introduced a fifth criterion beginning with the 16th letter of the alphabet.

Cut. Not the shape of the stone, cut refers to how well a diamond's facets are proportioned and aligned to maximize brilliance. According to Tiffany, an excellent cut might sacrifice as much as 62 percent of a stone's total weight.

Color. A lack of color is a sign of quality, indicating fewer impurities. Diamonds lower in quality can look very faintly yellowish to a well-trained jeweler's eye.

Clarity. Virtually all diamonds contain minute flaws, called inclusions, that diminish clarity. Those judged "flawless" (rated FL) show no visible inclusions under 10X magnification. Good-quality stones may also be rated IF (internally flawless with only minor surface inclusions), VVS1–VVS2 (very, very slightly included), or VS1–VS2 (very slightly included).

Carat Weight. One carat weighs 0.20 grams, with each carat equal to 100 "points." (A 50-point diamond, for example, could also be said to weigh half a carat.) While carat weight determines a stone's price to some degree, it cannot be judged without reference to the other three C's, since a small, beautifully cut, colorless, flawless stone could be worth far more than a larger stone of less brilliance or purity.

Presence. An addition to the judging process by Tiffany & Co., this takes into account such other qualities as the diamond's precision of cut, its symmetry, and its polish, all of which contribute to the overall visual impact of the stone.

AUSPICIOUS HINDU WEDDING GIFTS

♥♥♥

Whole numbers ending in "1" are considered to bring good fortune in the Hindu faith. Guests at traditional Indian weddings therefore present gifts in monetary support of the new couple, always making sure that their check or cash, whether rupees, dollars, pounds, or other currency, totals a number such as 11, 51, 101, and so on.

JAPANESE SYMBOLIC WEDDING FOODS

▼▼▼

At the banquet following a traditional Japanese wedding ceremony, certain foods are served for their propitious symbolic meaning. (The number of items served should never total a multiple of the number four, *shi,* which sounds similar to the first syllable of a word for death.)

Adzuki beans and rice: The color of the bright red beans represents good fortune.

Clams: Presented to guests complete with both shell halves, the bivalves symbolize togetherness.

Fish: Served whole, fish are cooked with their heads touching their tails to form circles that represent eternity.

Konbu: Dried kelp is served because its name is similar to the last two syllables of the word for "joy," *yorokobu.*

Lobster: When cooked, the crustacean's shell turns deep red, a lucky color.

Salted herring roe: The preserved fish eggs symbolize fertility.

Sea bream: This particular fish is served because its Japanese name, *tai,* is the last syllable of the word for happiness, *medetai.*

NO BETTER LOT IN LIFE

▼▼▼

I was once congratulating a friend, who had around him a blooming family, knit together in the strongest affection. "I can wish you no better lot," said he, with enthusiasm, "than to have a wife and children. If you are prosperous, there they are to share your prosperity; if otherwise, there they are to comfort you." And, indeed, I have observed that a married man falling into misfortune, is more apt to retrieve his situation in the world than a single one; partly, because he is more stimulated to exertion by the necessities of the helpless and beloved beings who depend upon him for subsistence, but chiefly because his spirits are soothed and relieved by domestic endearments, and his self-respect kept alive by finding, that, though all abroad is darkness and humiliation, yet there is still a little world of love at home, of which he is the monarch. Whereas, a single man is apt to run to waste and self-neglect; to fancy himself lonely and abandoned, and his heart to fall to ruin, like some deserted mansion, for want of an inhabitant.

—"The Wife" from *The Sketchbook of Geoffrey Crayon*
(1819–1820), Washington Irving

BRIDAL OUTFIT COLORS

▼▼

Married in **white**, you have chosen all right.
Married in **gray**, you will go far away.
Married in **black**, you will wish yourself back.
Married in **red**, you will wish yourself dead.
Married in **green**, ashamed to be seen.
Married in **blue**, love ever true.
Married in **pearl**, you will live in a whirl.
Married in **yellow**, ashamed of your fellow.
Married in **brown**, you will live out of town.
Married in **tan**, he will be a good man.
Married in **pink**, your spirits will sink.
[Alternatively, Married in **pink**, of you he will think.]
—19th century English folk rhyme

RANDOM STATS, PART I

▼▼

3 to 4 months: Average time ahead of wedding American bridesmaids' dresses are bought.
180: Average number of guests at an American wedding.
33 percent: Couples who hire a wedding consultant.
67 percent: Brides who continue to wear their wedding-day scent.

WEIRD LAWS: SINGLE LIFE

▼▼

A random compendium of archaic or just plain strange wedding-related laws still on the books. (See also "Weird Laws: Courtship," page 82; "Weird Laws: Weddings," page 125; and "Weird Laws: Married Life," page 166.)

Marry or don't jump! In the state of Florida, unmarried women may not go parachuting on a Sunday.
Marry or pay! The state of Missouri requires that single men aged 21 to 50 years pay an annual $1 tax.
Marry or don't fish! Unmarried women may not fish alone in the state of Montana.

THE MARRIED WOMEN'S PROPERTY ACT, 1849

▼▼

An act for the more effectual protection of the property of married women:

§1. The real property of any female who may hereafter marry, and which she shall own at the time of marriage, and the rents, issues, and profits thereof, shall not be subject to the sole disposal of her husband, nor be liable for his debts, and shall continue her sole and separate property, as if she were a single female.

§2. The real and personal property, and the rents, issues, and profits thereof, of any female now married, shall not be subject to the disposal of her husband; but shall be her sole and separate property, as if she were a single female, except so far as the same may be liable for the debts of her husband heretofore contracted.

§3. Any married female may take by inheritance, or by gift, grant, devise, or bequest, from any person other than her husband, and hold to her sole and separate use, and convey and devise real and personal property, and any interest or estate therein, and the rents, issues, and profits thereof, in the same manner and with like effect as if she were unmarried, and the same shall not be subject to the disposal of her husband nor be liable for his debts.

Note: While other laws had previously been passed giving married women some control of their property, this statute of New York State, enacted in 1848 and printed here as amended the following year, was the first to give them more comprehensive control.

UNIVERSAL TRUTH

▼▼

It is a truth universally acknowledged that a single man in possession of a good fortune must be in want of a wife.

However little known the feelings or views of such a man may be on his first entering a neighbourhood, this truth is so well fixed in the minds of the surrounding families that he is considered as the rightful property of some one or other of their daughters.

—Opening lines of *Pride and Prejudice* (1813), Jane Austen

SOME ROMANTIC MOVIES

▼▼

To pass the time or get in the mood while planning or waiting for the wedding, here's an arbitrary selection of some perennial favorites available on video or DVD. (See also "Some Wedding Movies," page 112–115.)

Gone with the Wind (1939): Vivien Leigh plays Scarlett O'Hara and Clark Gable is Rhett Butler, amid the tragic pageantry of the Civil War.

> *"I can't go all my life waiting to catch you between husbands."*
> —From the screenplay by Sidney Howard and others,
> based on the novel by Margaret Mitchell

The Shop Around the Corner (1940): Coworkers in a small Budapest shop, Jimmy Stewart and Margaret Sullavan fall in love as anonymous pen pals while disliking each other in person.

Casablanca (1942): Humphrey Bogart and Ingrid Bergman love passionately and nobly in Paris and Morocco during World War II.

Adam's Rib (1949): Real-life lovers Katharine Hepburn and Spencer Tracy play husband-and-wife lawyers battling it out in the courtroom.

> *"Lawyers should never marry other lawyers. This is called in-breeding;*
> *from this comes idiot children—and other lawyers."*
> —From the screenplay by Ruth Gordon and Garson Kanin

Roman Holiday (1953): Incognito princess Audrey Hepburn and incognito reporter Gregory Peck fall for each other in the Eternal City.

Sabrina (1954): Wealthy brothers Humphrey Bogart and William Holden vie for the love of a chauffeur's daughter, played by Audrey Hepburn.

An Affair to Remember (1957): Cary Grant and Deborah Kerr star as strangers who fall in love on an ocean liner, agree to meet six months later, and are almost kept tragically apart.

> *"There must be something between us, even if it's only an ocean."*
> —From the screenplay by Leo McCarey and Delmer Daves

Breakfast at Tiffany's (1961): Party girl Audrey Hepburn and struggling writer George Peppard find unlikely love in Manhattan.

Doctor Zhivago (1965): Omar Sharif plays the title role and Julie Christie his true love, Lara, in this epic set against the Russian Revolution.

> *"Good marriages are made in heaven . . . or some such place."*
> —From the screenplay by Robert Bolt

Romeo and Juliet (1968): Young English actors Leonard Whiting and Olivia Hussey play Shakespeare's star-crossed lovers in this opulent film.

Somewhere in Time (1980): Playwright Christopher Reeve hypnotically time-travels back seven decades to connect with true love Jane Seymour.

An Officer and a Gentleman (1982): Navy flyer and officer candidate Richard Gere does bad and good by factory worker Deborah Winger.

Dirty Dancing (1987): Patrick Swayze teaches naïve teen Jennifer Grey how to dance and love at a Catskills family camp.

The Princess Bride (1987): Wacky comedy combines with romance as stable boy/pirate Cary Elwes rescues true love/princess Robin Wright.

When Harry Met Sally (1989): Billy Crystal and Meg Ryan meet, hate each other, and then learn to love each other.

> *"I came here tonight because when you realize you want to spend the rest of your life with somebody, you want the rest of your life to start as soon as possible."*
> —From the screenplay by Nora Ephron

Pretty Woman (1990): L.A. "working girl" Julia Roberts undergoes a Cinderella transformation in a romance with tycoon Richard Gere.

Sleepless in Seattle (1993): Widower Tom Hanks and single gal Meg Ryan fall in love long-distance after she hears him on late-night radio.

> *"Marriage is hard enough without bringing such low expectations into it."*
> —From the screenplay by Nora Ephron

The American President (1995): Lobbyist Annette Bening and widower U.S. President Michael Douglas are hesitantly drawn to each other against a backdrop of political scheming.

While You Were Sleeping (1995): Sandra Bullock pretends to be the fiancée of a man in a coma, Peter Gallagher, then finds herself attracted to his brother, Bill Pullman.

Titanic (1997): Steerage passenger Leonardo DiCaprio and first-class voyager Kate Winslet find true love just before the great ocean liner sinks into the Atlantic.

Shakespeare in Love (1998): Young noblewoman Gwyneth Paltrow masquerades as a male actor while winning the heart of young Will, Joseph Fiennes, amidst the delightful maelstrom of theatrical life in late 16th century London.

> *"Love knows nothing of rank or riverbank."*
> —From the screenplay by Marc Norman and Tom Stoppard

Notting Hill (1999): Shy British bookstore owner Hugh Grant and top American movie star Julia Roberts fall in love in one of London's most charming neighborhoods.

> *"I'm also just a girl, standing in front of a boy, asking him to love her."*
> —From the screenplay by Richard Curtis

Moulin Rouge (2001): Courtesan Nicole Kidman and aspiring writer Ewan McGregor sing modern pop songs as they woo and break each other's heart in 1890s Paris.

Love Actually (2003): A kaleidoscope of romances merrily intertwine in modern London, starring Hugh Grant, Liam Neeson, Laura Linney, Emma Thompson, Colin Firth, Keira Knightly, and many others.

> *"Beautiful Aurelia, I've come here with a view of asking you to marriage me. I know I seems an insane person—because I hardly knows you—but sometimes things are so transparency, they don't need evidential proof."*
> —From the screenplay by Richard Curtis

SOME ITALIAN WEDDING CUSTOMS

▼▼▼

Masciata: In times past, this "message" of proposal would be carried by a matchmaker to the family of the intended bride, in the hopes that they would consent to a marriage.

Dote: This "bundle" was the trousseau assembled by the bride, containing household items and her clothing.

Public challenges: While the bride walked through town to her wedding, locals would place in her path various obstacles—a broom, a beggar, a crying child—intended to foretell the kind of wife she might become. If she picked up the broom, it meant she would keep a good home; if she treated the beggar kindly, she would live a charitable life; and if she comforted the crying child, she would be a good mother.

Groom's flowers: Especially in the north, the groom and his family may select the bouquet and bring it to the church to greet the bride when she arrives.

Toc ferro: A piece of iron is carried by the groom in his pocket as a talisman against the evil eye.

A shattered glass: To conclude their wedding ceremony, bride and groom may smash a glass or vase together, and the number of broken pieces is meant to signify the number of years of happy marriage they will enjoy together.

Sawing the log: A small-town tradition calls for husband and wife to saw a log in half together using a two-handled saw, symbolizing the way they will work together in facing all of life's challenges.

Bomboniera: These confetti-like bonbons, almonds sugar-coated in white as a sign of purity, signify life's combination of bitterness and sweetness. In tulle packets containing a lucky odd number, usually five pieces, these are tossed at the just-married couple to ensure that they have many children.

Per cen'tanni: A traditional wedding toast, "for a hundred years," is offered to the bride and groom with drinks passed around by the best man.

Money bag: The bride carries this satin bag, called *borsa* or *busta*, to receive gifts of money at the reception.

Cutting the tie: A popular northern tradition, this involves the best man cutting the groom's tie into pieces that he sells to wedding guests, raising money to pay or tip the band.

WOOSTERISMS ON "THE LONG JOURNEY TOGETHER"

▼♥

With the characters of Bertie Wooster and Jeeves, British comic novelist P. G. Wodehouse (1881–1975) captured a world of privileged young English nitwits and the wise menservants who looked after them. Most plots of the novels and short stories featuring narrator Bertie and his fellow members of London's Drones Club involve their elaborate machinations to pursue young women who are far brighter and more calculating than they, all the while avoiding marriage. Not surprisingly, these delightful tales feature many euphemisms for fiancés and fiancées, grooms and brides, engagements, weddings and marriages, and the married life that inevitably follows. Herewith, an arbitrary sampling.

Fiancé(s)/Groom(s)
flitting sipper [JIM]
other half of the sketch [SULJ]
partner of joys and sorrows [JFS]

Fiancée(s)/Bride(s)
other party in the matter [VGJ]
some tough babies [JIM]
tigress that has marked down its prey [COJ]

Engagement(s)
award the biscuit [JIM]
contracting a matrimonial alliance [VGJ]
Cupid's dart had done its stuff [JIM]
fearful predicament [JIM]
headed for the altar rails [JIM, JFS]
hit it off like ham and eggs [RHJ]
hitched up [JIM]
laughing Love God has been properly up on his toes [JIM]
one round of excitement [TYJ]
pending merger [JIM]
peril which must always loom [JFS]
projected union [JIM]
push his nose past the judges' box [RHJ]

reaching out for the nearest girl and slapping my soul
down in front of her RHJ
satisfactory settlement VGJ
signing her up SULJ
some idea of a union JIM
start pricing fish slices RHJ
starting on the long journey together JFS
trying to grab the gold ring on a merry-go-round RHJ
understanding TIJ, VGJ

Wedding(s)
bells . . . ring out in the little village church JIM
Bishop and colleague had done their stuff TCN
bought a buttonhole and went to it TIJ
curse JIM
enter upon that holy state TIJ
fusing of her soul with mine RHJ
get jugged JIM
leap in among the orange blossoms JIM
saunter down the aisle RHJ
scaffold JIM
signed on the dotted line VGJ
take her for better or for worse, as the book of rules puts it SULJ
teaming up TCN
walk upstairs with the little missus and collect the blessing TIJ

Marriage/Married Life
absolutely hitched up TIJ
after the clergyman had done his stuff JFS
essential balance VGJ
helping themselves to sausages out of the same dish
day after day at the breakfast sideboard RHJ
honourable state VGJ

Sources: COJ: *Carry On, Jeeves* (1925). JFS: *Jeeves and the Feudal Spirit* (1954). JIM: *Jeeves in the Morning* (1971). RHJ: *Right Ho, Jeeves* (1934). SULJ: *Stiff Upper Lip, Jeeves* (1962). TCN: *The Cat-Nappers* (1974). TIJ: *The Inimitable Jeeves* (1923). TYJ: *Thank You, Jeeves* (1933, 1934). VGJ: *Very Good, Jeeves!* (1930).

VOWS FOR LATE IN LIFE

♥♥

"Yes; it is evening with us now; and we have realized none of our morning dreams of happiness. But let us join our hands before the altar, as lovers whom adverse circumstances have separated through life, yet who meet again as they are leaving it, and find their earthly affection changed into something holy as religion. And what is Time, to the married of Eternity?"

—"The Wedding Knell" (1836), Nathaniel Hawthorne

POPULAR DIAMOND SHAPES

♥♥

In addition to selecting a stone based on the classic quality criteria (see "The Four C's (and One P) of Diamonds," page 14), the bride and groom should consider which is their preferred and most flattering shape in a cut diamond.

Emerald: Also known as a step cut, for its broad, flat facets, this elegant shape is rectangular, with beveled corners. Though less dazzling overall than rounder shapes, it can impress nonetheless as its broad facets catch the light. Good for larger hands or for brides who favor old-fashioned style.

Heart: Rotate a teardrop or pear shape 180 degrees and cut into its top a cleft, perfectly rounded on either side, and you get this shape, perfect for an especially romantic or sentimental bride.

Marquise: Commissioned by King Louis XIV of France and named in honor of the Marquise de Pompadour, whose bewitching smile reputedly inspired its alluring oval form with pointed ends, this shape, typically with 56 facets, looks especially good as a solitaire stone, and also flatters small hands or short fingers.

Oval: A slender, elongated shape, generally with 56 facets, that flatters short fingers or small hands, often set with two small matching diamonds on either side. Developed in the 1960s, this is now the third most popular diamond shape, suited to many different sizes and shapes of hand.

Pear: Poignantly resembling a teardrop, this shape, typically with 58 facets, resembles a marquise at one end and an oval at the other. It is an excellent choice for small to medium hands, and it is also frequently used for earrings or pendants.

Princess: A more modern cut, this square shape, which typically has

76 facets, can appear just as dazzling as a round brilliant and looks good on long fingers. Widely versatile and flattering, it is the second most popular diamond shape

Radiant: A hybrid of emerald and round brilliant, this rectangular or square shape with rounded corners dazzles with 62 to 70 facets. A versatile choice.

Round Brilliant: Its 58 facets give this perfectly circular stone its dazzling appearance, making it the most popular and widely flattering cut, accounting for approximately three-quarters of all diamonds sold.

Trilliant or Trillion: Taking its name from its triangular shape and dazzling brilliance, this unconventional shape for the more adventurous bride was first developed in Amsterdam. It may have sharply pointed or more gently rounded corners.

SOME HAWAIIAN WEDDING CUSTOMS

♥♥

Conch-shell fanfare: To begin the ceremony, someone blows a conch shell three times to summon the divine presence.

Leis: The groom wears a *lei*, the traditional Hawaiian floral necklace, made of fragrant, spear-shaped green *maile* leaves, interwoven with blossoms of *pikake* (white jasmine) and delicate orange petals of *ilima* flowers. The bride wears pure white *pikake* leis. In the most traditional of ceremonies, the bride's and groom's hands are bound together with leis.

Money dance *(pandango):* In this Filipino custom now popular at Hawaiian weddings regardless of ethnic origin, guests tuck money into or tape money to the bridal couple's clothing during their first dance.

Origami cranes *(tsurus):* In this Japanese custom, a crane folded from metallic origami paper is considered good luck in marriage, as cranes were believed to live for 1,000 years. The auspicious number of origami cranes for the couple is 1,001, with the bride and her bridesmaids traditionally folding 1,000 of them and the groom folding and adding the final crane. Wedding planners can arrange to have the cranes professionally folded and mounted for the bridal couple.

"Hawaiian Wedding Song": Popularized by Elvis Presley, this traditional tune will more often than not be sung, most likely accompanied by such traditional instruments as ukulele or slack-key guitar.

Fireworks and lion dance: Adopted from the Chinese immigrants to the islands, these two customs are also frequently incorporated into Hawaiian weddings to chase away evil spirits from the proceedings.

OUR WEDDING DAY

❤❤

In a year, in a year, when the grapes are ripe,
I shall stay no more away.
Then if you still are true, my love,
It will be our wedding day.
In a year, in a year, when my time is past,
Then I'll live in your love for aye.
Then if you still are true, my love,
It will be our wedding day.
—"Where the Trail Forks" (ca. 1900), Jack London

SOME JEWISH WEDDING CUSTOMS

▼▼▼

Ketubah: The traditional marriage contract, usually an ornately decorated document, is written in ancient Aramaic. Detailing the obligations of bride and groom to support each other, and signed by groom and bride, it is considered legally binding under Jewish law.

Bedecken: Veiling of the bride is believed to refer specifically to the first meeting of Rebecca and Isaac in Genesis 24:64–65: "And Rebekah lifted up her eyes, and when she saw Isaac, she lighted off the camel. For she had said unto the servant, What man is this that walketh in the field to meet us? And the servant had said, It is my master: therefore she took a veil, and covered herself." In this pre-wedding ceremony, the groom covers his bride's face with her veil, thus legally confirming her identity.

Chuppah: The cloth wedding canopy, held up by a pole at each of its four corners, dates back at least to the Middle Ages, when weddings were held outdoors and the canopy was used to create a special, separate place for the exchange of vows. It has come to symbolize the new home created by the joining of bride and groom.

Hakafot: This circling of the groom as the bride walks around him seven times represents not only his central role to her life but also the circle of sheltering love she will provide.

Shevah Berakhot: The rabbi recites seven traditional blessings over the newlyweds. (See "Seven Jewish Wedding Blessings," page 129.)

Breaking the glass: To conclude the ceremony, the groom smashes underfoot a wineglass wrapped in a cloth, after which guests yell "*Mazel tov!*"

(good luck!). This act may be taken to recall the destruction of the old temple in Jerusalem or the sorrow of Jewish exile, or to represent the fragility of life or the ending of old ways of life for the couple. In some ultra-contemporary Jewish weddings, the bride may also smash a glass.

Chair dance: During the wedding party, it is traditional for strong guests to dance while lifting both bride and groom, each holding one end of a scarf or napkin, into the air seated on chairs. This interpretation of the Talmudic teaching that guests must bring the couple joy literally elevates them to the status of queen and king at their celebration.

SOME *DICHOS Y REFRANES* ON WEDDINGS AND MARRIAGE

♥♥♥

One of the richest veins of Latino folk wisdom, Mexican and Southwestern *dichos* and *refranes*, literally "sayings" and "refrains," cover all aspects of life, including courtship, weddings, and marriages. Here are some examples of these pithy, often humorous, proverbs.

El amor es ciego, pero los vecinos no.
[Love is blind, but the neighbors aren't.]
♥

El matrimonio es como la muerte; pocos llegan a él preparados.
[Marriage is like death: few come to it prepared.]
♥

El amor es un juego; el matrimonio es un negocio.
[Love is a game; marriage is a negotiation.]
♥

El amor es ciego, pero el matrimonio le restaura la vista.
[Love is blind, but marriage restores your sight.]
♥

El melón y el casamiento ha de ser acertamiento.
[As with the melon, so the marriage: you have to be certain. (In other words, choose carefully.)]
♥

Busca arrepentimiento, el que busca casamiento.
[He seeks repentance, he who seeks marriage.]
♥

Para el gato viejo, un ratón tierno.
[For the old cat, a tender mouse. (This is said of an older man with a young bride.)]

BRIDAL SHOP NAMES

♥♥♥

A random survey of bridal shop names in the English-speaking world reveals some of the many ways people think about weddings.

Eternal Vows
Always and Forever
Eternity
Ever After
Everlasting Dreams
Forever After
Forever Yours
Forever Together
Happily Ever After
Immortal Beloved
Now and Forever

By the Numbers
2 Cute
4Everafter
A-1 Discount
Dress 2 the 9's
Jus' 4 U

Part of the Ceremony
Altar Bound
Down the Aisle
From This Day Forward
Here Comes the Bride
I Do! I Do!
Kiss the Bride
Repeat After Me
To Have and To Hold
With This Ring

The Empowered Bride
Be Confident, Be Beautiful
Beautiful Day
Classy Lady
Her Own Woman
It's Your Day
Not Always a Bridesmaid

Perfect Bride
Savvy Bride

A Family Affair
Daddy's Little Girl
Just Like Mom's
My Daughter's Wedding

Magic and Fantasy
Abracadabra
Busy Elves
Cinderella
Dragon's Blood Creations
Enchanted Cottage
Enchanted Hearts
Enchanting Elegance
Fairy Godmothers
Fairytales
Gingerbread House
Glass Slipper
Lady of the Lake
Magic Dream
Magic Moments
Magic Wand
Once Upon a Dream
Storybook Weddings

No-Nonsense
Better Wedding Bureau
Bridal Barn
Bridal Express
Hitching Post
One Stop
Wedding Sense

A Nod to the Groom
Belles & Beaus

Between Two Hearts
Connecting Two Hearts
He Loves Me!
Hearts Entwined
Just Because He Cares
Marry Me
Two of Hearts

Puns and Wordplay
Bridal Veil Falls
Bridal Path
Bride Ideas
Dreamoments
Field of Seams
Marry Merry
Marrymakers
Sew Many Weddings
Sewly Yours & Once Upon a Bride
Vow Wows
Wedding Belles

An Air of Romance
Bride's Dream
Destiny's Bride
Dream Maker's
Juliet's Balcony
Kissing Moon
Lover's Lane
Misty Eyes
Ribbon of Love
Sweet Beginnings
Swept Away
Vive L'Amour

The Royal Touch
Fit for a Queen
Lady Di's
Princess
Royale Weddings

Something . . . Or Other
Something Blue
Something Borrowed Etc.

Something Borrowed Something Blue
Something Borrowed Something New
Something Knew
Something Old Something New
Somethings Borrowed
Something's Old Something's New

Song and Screen
All About Eve
Dream Weaver
Just Begun
Love Story
My Fair Lady
Nights in White Satin
Pretty Woman
Ruby Slippers
We've Only Just Begun
White Lace & Promises

A Spiritual Event
Angels on Clouds
Blessing Moments
Blessings
God's Original Designs
Heavenly
A Heavenly Celebration
Holy Matrimony

Natural Allusions
Baby's Breath
Honey Bee
Petals & Promises
Rainbow
Red Frogs & Tall Poppies
Turtle Dove

A Touch of Attitude
Billion $ Dreams
Jealousy
Pizazz!
Poor Little Rich Girl
Sassy's

SOME AFRICAN HERITAGE WEDDING TRADITIONS

♥♥

Braiding: Throughout Africa, traditional brides and grooms may have their hair elaborately braided to mark the special occasion. Couples of African heritage may wish to observe their weddings in a similar way.

Carrying fire: Traditional South African weddings may feature the parents of the wedding couple carrying glowing embers from their own hearths during the processional, to be used for lighting the hearth of the newlyweds' home. In modern African heritage weddings, these could be replaced by candles, and a unity candle (see page 58) could symbolically stand in for the newlyweds' hearth.

Colors: Vibrant African patterns, particularly in traditional colors such as red, black, and green, may be incorporated into both bride's and groom's wedding attire.

Cowrie shells: These beautiful little shells, an ancient form of money in West Africa, may be used to adorn the bride as a symbol of good fortune, whether as jewelry or sewn on as decorations for the wedding gown.

Drums: Long a part of African tradition, rhythmic drumming may be incorporated into an African heritage wedding, either as an accompaniment to the processional or recessional, or as part of the celebration to follow.

Jumping the broom: People of many diverse cultures besides those of Africa—including Scotland, Hungary, and Gypsy cultures—include brooms among wedding rituals, particularly as a playful symbol of the bride's housekeeping abilities and of the couple's setting up a new home together. But for African Americans the tradition has deeper, more poignant meaning. It harks back to pre–Civil War days, when slaves in the South were forbidden to marry, and the old African ritual of jumping over a broom together became a way of formalizing the commitment between a man and woman, marking their "leap" into a new life together. In modern African American weddings, couples may jump over the broom either to begin the ceremony or to conclude it after they've been formally pronounced husband and wife.

REGAL SILVER GOWNS

♥♥

Until Queen Victoria set a new trend by wearing a white gown for her February 10, 1840, marriage to Prince Albert, British royalty traditionally wore silver gowns on their wedding day.

RANDOM STATS, PART II: AMERICAN ATTITUDES TO MARRIAGE
▼▼▼

Some figures from "The State of Our Unions," a 2004 report from The National Marriage Project at Rutgers, The State University of New Jersey:

9.5 million: American married men between the ages of 25 and 34 years, as of 2002.

63 percent: Married men who, when they were 15, lived with both of their biological parents.

15 percent: Married men who believe that men married at an earlier age than they wanted because their wives pushed them to.

35 percent: Married men who agree with the belief that you marry to have children.

75 percent: Married men who say they specifically looked for someone who would be a good mother when choosing a wife.

94 percent: American men who say they are happier married than single.

83 percent: American teenage girls who say that a good marriage and family life are "extremely important."

72 percent: American teenage boys who say that a good marriage and family life are "extremely important."

A HEARTFELT BRIDAL VOW
▼▼▼

> If ever two were one, then surely we.
> If ever man were lov'd by wife, then thee;
> If ever wife was happy in a man,
> Compare with me ye women if you can.
> I prize thy love more than whole Mines of gold,
> Or all the riches that the East doth hold.
> My love is such that Rivers cannot quench,
> Nor ought but love from thee, give recompence.
> Thy love is such I can no way repay,
> The heavens reward the manifold I pray.
> Then while we live, in love lets so persever,
> That when we live no more, we may live ever.
> —"To My Dear and Loving Husband" (1650), Anne Bradstreet

CLASSIC AND CONTEMPORARY FIRST-DANCE SONGS

♥♥♥

Use the following list to help you pick just the right romantic song for the first dance—or an entire play list for your wedding party DJ.

Title	Artist
Against All Odds	Phil Collins
All I Ask of You	Michael Crawford
All My Life	Linda Ronstadt and Aaron Neville
All the Way	Frank Sinatra
Always	Frank Sinatra
Always on My Mind	Willie Nelson
And I Love Her	The Beatles
Annie's Song	John Denver
As Time Goes By	Jimmy Durante
At Last	Etta James
Beautiful	Gordon Lightfoot
Beauty and The Beast	Celine Dion and Peabo Bryson
Because You Loved Me	Celine Dion
Can I Have This Dance?	Ann Murray
Can You Feel The Love Tonight?	Elton John
Can't Fight This Feeling	REO Speedwagon
Can't Get Enough of Your Love	Barry White
Can't Help Falling in Love	Elvis Presley
Can't Take My Eyes Off of You	Frankie Valli
Caught Up in the Rapture	Anita Baker
Chances Are	Johnny Mathis
Cherish	The Association
Cherish (the Love)	Kool and The Gang
Close to You	The Carpenters
Colour My World	Chicago
Come Rain or Come Shine	Bette Midler
Don't Know Much	Linda Ronstadt and Aaron Neville
Dream a Little Dream of Me	The Mamas and The Papas
Embraceable You	Frank Sinatra
Endless Love	Diana Ross and Lionel Richie
Eternal Flame	The Bangles
Everybody Loves Somebody	Dean Martin

Title	Artist
Everything I Do (I Do for You)	Bryan Adams
First Time Ever I Saw Your Face	Roberta Flack
Fly Me to the Moon	Frank Sinatra
For Once in My Life	Stevie Wonder
Forever	Nat King Cole
Forever and Ever, Amen	Randy Travis
Friends	Elton John
Giving You the Best That I Got	Anita Baker
Glory of Love	Peter Cetera
Happy Together	The Turtles
Have I Told You Lately	Rod Stewart
Hawaiian Wedding Song	Elvis Presley
Hello	Lionel Richie
Here and Now	Luther Vandross
Here, There, and Everywhere	The Beatles
Hold Me, Thrill Me, Kiss Me	Mel Carter
How Do I Live	Trisha Yearwood
How Sweet It Is	James Taylor
I Can't Help Falling in Love	Elvis Presley
I Can't Stop Loving You	Ray Charles
I Cross My Heart	George Strait
I Finally Found Someone	Barbara Streisand and Bryan Adams
I Get a Kick Out of You	Frank Sinatra
I Got You Babe	Sonny and Cher
I Love the Way You Love Me	John Michael Montgomery
I Only Have Eyes for You	The Flamingos
I Swear	John Michael Montgomery
I Want to Know What Love Is	Foreigner
I Will Always Love You	Whitney Houston
I'll Stand by You	The Pretenders
Islands in the Stream	Dolly Parton and Kenny Rogers
I've Got You Under My Skin	Frank Sinatra
If	Bread
In My Life	The Beatles
In Your Eyes	Peter Gabriel
Into the Mystic	Van Morrison
Is This Love	Bob Marley

Title	Artist
Just the Way You Are	Billy Joel
Killing Me Softly	Roberta Flack
Kiss from a Rose	Seal
L-O-V-E	Nat King Cole
Lady	Kenny Rogers
Let It Be Me	The Everly Brothers
Let's Stay Together	Al Green
Longer	Dan Fogelberg
Love and Marriage	Frank Sinatra
Love Me Tender	Elvis Presley
Love Will Keep Us Alive	The Eagles
Love Will Keep Us Together	Captain and Tenille
Loving You	Elvis Presley
Maybe I'm Amazed	Paul McCartney
Misty	Johnny Mathis
Moonlight Serenade	Glenn Miller Orchestra
My Cherie Amour	Stevie Wonder
My Girl	The Temptations
My Heart Will Go On	Celine Dion
Never Gonna Let You Go	Sergio Mendes and Brasil '66
Never My Love	The Association
Night and Day	Frank Sinatra
No Ordinary Love	Sade
Only You	The Platters
Ooh Baby, Baby	Linda Ronstadt
Open Arms	Journey
Our Love Is Here to Stay	Frank Sinatra
Sea of Love	Phil Phillips and The Twilights
She's Got a Way	Billy Joel
Shining Star	The Manhattans
Since I Fell for You	Lenny Welch
Solid (As a Rock)	Ashford and Simpson
Something	The Beatles
Sometimes When We Touch	Dan Hill
Stand By Me	Ben E. King
Stardust	Nat King Cole
Suddenly	Billy Ocean
Sweet Love	Anita Baker

Title	Artist
Take My Breath Away	Berlin
Tell It Like It Is	Aaron Neville
This Guy's In Love with You	Herb Alpert and The Tijuana Brass
Three Times a Lady	The Commodores
Through the Eyes of Love	Melissa Manchester
Through the Fire	Chaka Khan
Through the Years	Kenny Rogers
To Make You Feel My Love	Garth Brooks
Tonight I Celebrate My Love	Roberta Flack and Peabo Bryson
True Companion	Marc Cohn
Truly, Madly, Deeply	Savage Garden
Try a Little Tenderness	Otis Redding
Twelfth of Never	Johnny Mathis
Unchained Melody	The Righteous Brothers
Unforgettable	Nat King Cole
Up Where We Belong	Joe Cocker and Jennifer Warnes
Valentine	Jim Brickman and Martina McBride
Way You Look Tonight, The	Frank Sinatra
Wedding Song (There Is Love)	Paul Stookey (see also page 76)
We're In This Love Together	Al Jarreau
We've Only Just Begun	The Carpenters
What a Wonderful World	Louis Armstrong
When a Man Loves a Woman	Percy Sledge
When I Fall in Love	Nat King Cole
When You Say Nothing at All	Alison Krause
Whole New World, A	Peabo Bryson and Regina Bell
Wind Beneath My Wings	Bette Midler
With You I'm Born Again	Billy Preston and Syreeta Wright
Wonderful Tonight	Eric Clapton
Wonderful Wonderful	Johnny Mathis
You and I	Crystal Gayle and Eddie Rabbitt
You are So Beautiful	Joe Cocker
You are the Sunshine of My Life	Stevie Wonder
You Light Up My Life	Debbie Boone
You Make Me Feel So Young	Frank Sinatra
You're Still the One	Shania Twain
Your Song	Elton John

FOR BRIDES IN WAITING: ENGAGEMENT RINGS

The first engagement rings, as items separate from wedding rings, came about in the 13th century after Pope Innocent III declared that Catholics observe a waiting period between betrothal and marriage.

THE CLAY OF MARRIAGE

You and I
Have so much love
That it
Burns like a fire,
In which we bake a lump of clay
Molded into a figure of you
And a figure of me.

Then we take both figures
And we break them into pieces,
And mix the pieces with water,
And mold once more a figure of you
And a figure of me.

I am in your clay.
You are in my clay.
In life we share a single quilt.
In death we will share one coffin.
—"You and I," Kuan Tao-Sheng (1262–1319)

MARRIAGE BY PROXY

Three states—Colorado, Montana, and Texas—currently allow marriage by proxy—that is, a marriage in which another person, legally designated in writing, stands in as the proxy for a bride or groom who cannot be present for good reason. Reasons may include military service, illness, or imprisonment. Certain jurisdictions in Canada allow marriage by proxy, and Mexico and Paraguay allow it by mail order.

VERY PROPER

♥♥♥

It was a very proper wedding. The bride was elegantly dressed; the two bridesmaids were duly inferior; her father gave her away; her mother stood with salts in her hand, expecting to be agitated; her aunt tried to cry; and the service was impressively read by Dr. Grant.

—*Mansfield Park* (1814), Jane Austen

THE NINE HUSBANDS OF ZSA ZSA GABOR

♥♥♥

The Hungarian-born femme fatale and actress spoke with authority when she came up with such signature quips as "I am a marvelous housekeeper. Every time I leave a man, I keep his house," "You never really know a man until you have divorced him," and "How many husbands have I had? You mean apart from my own?"

Zsa Zsa's husbands:

1. **Burhan Belge**, Turkish diplomat (1937–1941)
2. **Conrad Hilton**, hotelier (1942–1947)
3. **George Sanders**, actor (1949–1954)*
4. **Herbert Hunter**, financial consultant (1964–1966)
5. **Joshua S. Cosden, Jr.**, oilman (1966–1967)
6. **Jack Ryan**, toy inventor (1975–1976)
7. **Michael O'Hara**, divorce lawyer (1977–1982)
8. **Felipe de Alba**, playboy (1982)**
9. **Frederick Prinz von Anhalt**, prince (1986–)***

* Sanders later married Zsa Zsa's sister, Magda.

** Marriage lasted one day, annulled not only because Gabor was technically still married to O'Hara but also because, though conducted at sea, the vessel was not in international waters at the time.

*** Real name, Robert Lichtenberg; royal title purchased in adulthood.

A MAN'S POSITION

♥♥♥

Bridegroom! What a word! It makes a man realize his position, somehow.

—*Pygmalion* (1916), George Bernard Shaw

FROM THE SONG OF SONGS

▼♥

The voice of my beloved!
Behold, he cometh leaping upon the mountains,
Skipping upon the hills.
My beloved is like a roe or a young hart:
Behold, he standeth behind our wall,
He looketh forth at the windows,
Shewing himself through the lattice.
My beloved spake, and said unto me,
Rise up, my love, my fair one, and come away.
For, lo, the winter is past, the rain is over and gone;
The flowers appear on the earth;
The time of the singing of birds is come,
And the voice of the turtle is heard in our land;
The fig tree putteth forth her green figs,
And the vines with the tender grape give a good smell.
Arise, my love, my fair one, and come away.
(2:8–13)

Thou hast ravished my heart, my sister, my spouse;
Thou hast ravished my heart with one of thine eyes,
With one chain of thy neck.
How fair is thy love, my sister, my spouse!
How much better is thy love than wine!
And the smell of thine ointments than all spices!
Thy lips, O my spouse, drop as the honeycomb:
Honey and milk are under thy tongue.
(4:9–11)

Set me as a seal upon thine heart, as a seal upon thine arm:
For love is strong as death; jealousy is cruel as the grave:
The coals thereof are coals of fire, which hath a most vehement flame.
Many waters cannot quench love, neither can the floods drown it:
If a man would give all the substance of his house for love,
It would utterly be contemned.
(8: 6–7)

—The Holy Bible (King James Version)

SOME CHINESE WEDDING CUSTOMS

▼▼

Three letters: In traditional Chinese marriages, the nuptials are arranged through three formal letters sent between the families of bride and groom. First, a letter is sent with gifts to the bride's family, confirming that the marriage will take place. Second, a "gift letter" detailing the traditional wedding gifts it accompanies goes to the bride's family. Third, on the wedding day, the bride's family sends the groom's a letter confirming that the bride is becoming a member of their family.

Six etiquettes: These half-dozen customs must be observed: a request of marriage, verbally delivered to the bride's family by an elderly spokeswoman hired by the groom's family; a confirmation of birth dates by a fortune-teller, to ensure that the match is propitious; some token gifts for the bride's family, accompanying the gift letter (see above); some formal gifts for the bride's family to confirm the engagement, including offerings of savory and sweet foods for the spirits of ancestors; selection of an auspicious wedding date by the fortune-teller; and a wedding ceremony held in the groom's family home, with the couple dressed in red for good luck.

Red for good luck: As well as the bride's and groom's outfits, the color red appears on invitations, guest books, and other items to bring good fortune.

Shuang xi: The Chinese character pronounced "she" means happiness, and when doubled, to make *shuang xi*, it holds forth the promise of happiness for both bride and groom. The doubled character is a prominent decoration at the wedding ceremony or party.

Groom's gifts: Before the wedding, the bride gives the groom gifts for their new home, including kitchen equipment, bed linens, and jewelry.

Bridal bed: Several days before the wedding, a man and a woman who have both had happy marriages are hired to prepare the marital bed, positioning it in the most auspicious place in the bedroom and decorating its fresh linens with fruit to signify a fruitful life together.

Hair combing: On the eve of the wedding, the hair of both the bride and the groom is combed four times: once for a committed marriage, once for a harmonious life together, once to bring many male progeny, and a final time for a prosperous and long life together.

Tea ceremony: Bride and groom together perform a traditional tea ceremony, brewing a pot and serving first her parents and grandparents, then his.

The bride's return: Traditionally, the bride visits her parents three days after the wedding, bringing food and gifts to pay them tribute.

SOME CHARLES AND DIANA WEDDING MEMORABILIA

♥♥♥

Here is a brief survey of the hundreds of pieces of wedding memorabilia offered for sale on eBay commemorating the July 29, 1981, wedding of Britain's Prince Charles and Lady Diana Spencer, possibly the most publicized wedding in history.

- Bell, Sadler china
- Bottle opener, brass
- Bowl, Elizabethan bone china
- Bud vase, Mason's ironstone
- Button
- Champagne, Bollinger 1973 vintage (served at the wedding)
- Checklist of commemorative stamps
- Coca-Cola UK "Royal Wedding" bottle, unopened
- Coin, crown
- Decanter, Thomas Webb crystal
- Dishes, Wedgwood
- First day cover stamps
- Goblets
- Key ring, leather
- Lager, Welsh
- Loving cup, Royal Doulton
- LP record, official BBC coverage
- Magazine, *Australian Women's Weekly*
- Magazine, *Life*
- Magazine, *People*
- Magazine, *Radio Times*
- Magazine, *TV Guide*
- Medallion, framed
- Money box, Wedgwood
- Mug, Portmeirion
- Mug, Prinknash Pottery
- Mug, Spode
- Mug, Wedgwood
- Needlepoint tapestry
- Newspaper, *Daily Express*
- Ode, signed by Poet Laureate Sir John Betjeman
- Paperweight, glass with embedded postage stamp
- Paperweight, Welsh glass
- Place mats, set of six
- Playing cards, one Charles deck, one Diana deck
- Plate, Denby
- Plate, Mayfair fine bone china
- Plates, Coalport bone china
- Postcard
- Posters
- Programme, official
- Puzzle cube, "Rubik"-style
- Puzzle, jigsaw
- Spoon, silver plate
- Tankard, half-pint glass
- Tea caddy, Ridgways tea
- Tea jar, Sadler china
- Tea towel, linen
- Thimble, Spode
- Tickets, London Transport
- Tile
- Tray, Wedgwood
- Trinket box, heart-shaped, Carlton Ware
- Vacuum flask (Thermos)

FAREWELL TO BACHELOR BEHAVIOR!

♥♥♥

Anselmo was deep in love with a high-born and beautiful maiden of the same city, the daughter of parents so estimable, and so estimable herself, that he resolved, with the approval of his friend Lothario, without whom he did nothing, to ask her of them in marriage, and did so. . . . The first few days, those of a wedding being usually days of merry-making, Lothario frequented his friend Anselmo's house as he had been wont, striving to do honour to him and to the occasion, and to gratify him in every way he could; but when the wedding days were over and the succession of visits and congratulations had slackened, he began purposely to leave off going to the house of Anselmo, for it seemed to him, as it naturally would to all men of sense, that friends' houses ought not to be visited after marriage with the same frequency as in their masters' bachelor days.

—*Don Quixote* (1605, 1615), Miguel de Cervantes

WARTIME BRIDAL GOWNS

♥♥

During World War I and World War II, scarcity and rationing of fabric led brides to wear shorter wedding gowns or to forego gowns in favor of sensible skirt-and-jacket suits.

A PRESIDENTIAL PROPOSAL

♥♥

During the Great Depression, Harry Hopkins, Works Projects Administration head and a special assistant to President Franklin Delano Roosevelt, proposed to his love Louise Macy by telling her, "I was just talking to the president, and I asked him whether he thought you would say yes if I asked you to marry me, and the president said he thought you would."

Louise's reply: "As usual, the president was right."

A LONG CONVERSATION

♥♥

A happy marriage is a long conversation that always seems too short.

—André Maurois (1885–1967)

WEDDING CAKE SIZES AND SERVINGS

▼▼▼

Use the following charts to calculate the right wedding cake size. If the couple plans to save the top tier for their first anniversary, add 10 servings to the total.

YIELD PER TIER

Round Cake Diameter	Servings
6 inches	10
8 inches	18
9 inches	23
10 inches	29
12 inches	41
14 inches	56
16 inches	73
18 inches	93
20 inches	114
22 inches	138
24 inches	165

MULTIPLE-TIER CAKE YIELDS

Number of Guests	Tier Configuration (diameter, in inches)
16–19	8, 6
26–29	10, 6
23–30	10, 8
56–64	12, 8, 6
56–99	12, 9, 6
76–89	14, 10, 6
78–90	14, 10, 8
96–109	14, 10, 8, 6
103–125	16, 12, 8
121–144	16, 12, 8, 6
126–144	16, 12, 9, 6
146–184	18, 12, 10, 6
161–189	18, 14, 10, 6
198–230	20, 16, 12, 8
231–274	20, 16, 12, 9, 6
293–350	20, 18, 16, 12, 8
381–449	24, 20, 16, 12, 9, 6

TYING THE KNOT

♥♥

The popular euphemism for marriage, "tying the knot," comes from the old Irish custom known as "handfasting," in which the bride's and groom's hands were tied together during the marriage ceremony as a symbol of their commitment to each other. Symbolic knots are tied in other cultures as well, including the *sapta padi* ceremony in a Hindu wedding (page 71).

HAVE A *LORD OF THE RINGS* WEDDING

♥♥

The huge worldwide popularity of Peter Jackson's three-part film adaptation of *The Lord of the Rings* has added new fuel to a craze for Hobbit- and Elvish-inspired weddings that has existed since soon after the first publication of J. R. R. Tolkien's books on Middle Earth in the late 1930s. Some recent options:

Elvish invitations: Using the script devised by linguist Tolkien, wedding invitations, translated from the language of bride and groom, can be typeset and printed in Elvish (accompanied by translations for those who do not know the language).

Middle Earth jewelry: Bride and groom can exchange licensed replicas of jewelry from the movies, including the golden "one ring," the Evenstar pendant given by Arwen, the immortal Elf, to her human love Aragorn, and the leaf brooches worn by the Fellowship of the Ring.

Wedding attire: Gowns in the style of the movie costumes may frequently be found listed for sale on eBay.

Authentic settings: Wedding celebrations can now be arranged in some of the exact idyllic New Zealand countryside locations used for the movie.

Movie music: The Academy Award–winning score composed by Howard Shore, available on CD, is now being used by enthusiasts for their processional, recessional, or incidental music.

Middle Earth–inspired ceremony: Raleigh, North Carolina interfaith minister and Tolkien enthusiast Reverend Kara L. Mueller is at work devising a Tolkien-style ceremony inspired by "the mythology and beauty of Middle Earth." See her Web site, www.revkara.com, for more information.

SOME SCOTTISH WEDDING CUSTOMS

▼♥♥

Banns: Proclamations of the intended wedding are read aloud in the parish church for three successive Sundays.

Creeling the bridegroom: During a stag party a few days before the wedding, the groom's friends tie a creel, or basket, to his back and fill it with stones. He has to walk around the village with the creel on his back, to be rescued only by a kiss from his bride-to-be.

Showing presents: The bride's mother invites friends over to her home before the wedding for a display of the opened wedding presents that the couple has received.

Feet washing: At raucous festivities the night before the wedding, guests gather to wash the feet of the bride in a tub of hot water. Tradition says that whichever unmarried guest finds the ring of a married guest (which had been placed in the tub before filling) will be the next person to wed.

First foot: En route to the church, the first person to encounter the bride is rewarded with a coin and a drink of whisky and invited to join the procession.

First and second dances: The newlywed couple's first dance is traditionally a Scottish reel performed to a traditional piper's tune. The bride dances next with the most honored attending guest, based on social rank or age.

The scrammy: As the couple leaves the church, the groom and his friends scatter handfuls of coins in the churchyard, and local children scramble to pick them up.

Breaking the bannock: After the ceremony and before the bride is carried over the threshold by her groom, the traditional cake of barley or oat flour known as a bannock is broken over her head as a sign of good fortune, and pieces of it are passed around to guests.

THE HAND

♥▼♥▼♥▼♥▼♥▼♥▼♥▼♥▼♥▼♥▼♥▼♥▼♥▼♥▼♥▼♥▼♥▼♥▼♥▼♥♥

Laura turned her hand in the sunshine. The gold of the ring gleamed, the garnet glowed richly in the center of the flat, oval set, and on either side of it the pearls shimmered lustrously.

"It is beautiful, this ring," she said.

"I would say the hand," Almanzo replied.

—*These Happy Golden Years* (1943), Laura Ingalls Wilder

MARRIAGE ACROSS INTERNATIONAL BORDERS

▼▼

The 1975 Helsinki Agreement was a landmark in the political détente that helped lead to the downfall of Communism a decade and a half later. This Final Act of the 1975 Summit of the Conference for Security and Co-operation in Europe included language that facilitated marriages between citizens of different countries, a particularly groundbreaking measure for brides- or husbands-to-be who lived behind the Iron Curtain, under the influence of the Soviet Union.

Countries that ratified the Agreement in Helsinki on August 1, 1975, were Austria, Belgium, Bulgaria, Canada, Cyprus, Czechoslovakia, Denmark, Finland, France, the German Democratic Republic, the Federal Republic of Germany, Greece, the Holy See, Hungary, Iceland, Ireland, Italy, Liechtenstein, Luxembourg, Malta, Monaco, the Netherlands, Norway, Poland, Portugal, Romania, San Marino, Spain, Sweden, Switzerland, Turkey, the Union of Soviet Socialist Republics, the United Kingdom, the United States of America, and Yugoslavia.

Marriage between Citizens of Different States

The participating States will examine favourably and on the basis of humanitarian considerations requests for exit or entry permits from persons who have decided to marry a citizen from another participating State.

The processing and issuing of the documents required for the above purposes and for the marriage will be in accordance with the provisions accepted for family reunification.

In dealing with requests from couples from different participating States, once married, to enable them and the minor children of their marriage to transfer their permanent residence to a State in which either one is normally a resident, the participating States will also apply the provisions accepted for family reunification.

WHEN ONE GOWN IS NOT ENOUGH

▼▼

Some upscale brides are now buying not one wedding gown but two: one designed in traditional style to wear during the ceremony and a second cut in a trendier fashion to change into for the wedding party.

BEST MATCHES ACCORDING TO THE CHINESE ZODIAC

♥♥♥

The Chinese zodiac, developed more than 3,000 years ago, designates personality traits based on the year in which a person is born. Each year is represented by one of 12 animal signs. Though each sign is more or less compatible with other particular signs, other factors come into play. In other words, do not let your particular Chinese zodiac signs make or break your marriage plans! (*Note:* If your birthday falls in late January or early February, you'll have to do additional research to determine your sign, as the Chinese New Year falls on a different date at that time each year.)

RAT: 1924, 1936, 1948, 1960, 1972, 1984, 1996, 2008, 2020, 2032, 2044
Positive marriage traits: Creative, generous, charming.
Best matches: Dragon, Monkey.
Least compatible: Horse.

❦

OX: 1925, 1937, 1949, 1961, 1973, 1985, 1997, 2009, 2021, 2033, 2045
Positive marriage traits: Inspiring, relaxed, straightforward.
Best matches: Snake, Rooster.
Least compatible: Sheep.

❦

TIGER: 1926, 1938, 1950, 1962, 1974, 1986, 1998, 2010, 2022, 2034, 2046
Positive marriage traits: Emotional, sensitive, loving.
Best matches: Horse, Dog.
Least compatible: Monkey.

❦

RABBIT: 1927, 1939, 1951, 1963, 1975, 1987,
1999, 2011, 2023, 2035, 2047
Positive marriage traits: Affectionate, pleasant, calm.
Best matches: Sheep, Pig.
Least compatible: Rooster.

❦

DRAGON: 1928, 1940, 1952, 1964, 1976, 1988,
2000, 2012, 2024, 2036, 2048
Positive marriage traits: Vital, enthusiastic, softhearted.
Best matches: Snake, Rooster.
Least compatible: Sheep.

❦

SNAKE: 1929, 1941, 1953, 1965, 1977, 1989, 2001, 2013, 2025, 2037, 2049.
Positive marriage traits: Romantic, charming, intuitive.
Best matches: Ox, Rooster.
Least compatible: Pig.
❦

HORSE: 1930, 1942, 1954, 1966, 1978, 1990, 2002, 2014, 2026, 2038, 2050.
Positive marriage traits: Hardworking, friendly, intelligent.
Best matches: Tiger, Dog.
Least compatible: Rat.
❦

SHEEP: 1931, 1943, 1955, 1967, 1979, 1991, 2003, 2015, 2027, 2039, 2051.
Positive marriage traits: Passionate, creative, charming.
Best matches: Rabbit, Pig.
Least compatible: Ox.
❦

MONKEY: 1932, 1944, 1956, 1968, 1980, 1992, 2004, 2016, 2028, 2040, 2052.
Positive marriage traits: Intelligent, witty, entertaining.
Best matches: Rat, Dragon.
Least compatible: Tiger.
❦

ROOSTER: 1933, 1945, 1957, 1969, 1981, 1993, 2005, 2017, 2029, 2041, 2053.
Positive marriage traits: Scholarly, shrewd, decisive.
Best matches: Ox, Snake.
Least compatible: Rabbit.
❦

DOG: 1934, 1946, 1958, 1970, 1982, 1994, 2006, 2018, 2030, 2042, 2054.
Positive marriage traits: Honest, faithful, generous.
Best matches: Tiger, Horse.
Least compatible: Dragon.
❦

PIG: 1935, 1947, 1959, 1971, 1983, 1995, 2007, 2019, 2031, 2043, 2055.
Positive marriage traits: Sincere, loving, companionable.
Best matches: Rabbit, Sheep.
Least compatible: Pig.

SOME IRISH WEDDING CUSTOMS
♥♥♥

Bells: Rung to chase off evil spirits, small bells may be passed out among the congregants to be sounded as the bride walks down the aisle.

Magic hanky: The bride carries a special linen handkerchief that later can be simply transformed with needle and thread into a bonnet for her first baby.

Horseshoes: Dating back to the ancient belief that the iron from which actual horseshoes are forged has magical powers, this tradition calls for the bride to carry a tiny horseshoe charm in her bouquet or sewn into the hem of her dress as a symbol of good fortune. Bride and groom may also be given an actual horseshoe as a gift, to hang in their home together. Horseshoes are always placed with their open ends facing up so that fortune won't spill out.

Handfasting: Source of a popular euphemism for weddings (see "Tying the Knot," page 43), this ancient Celtic ceremony involved the tying together of a couple's wrists as a symbol of their unity, sometimes without benefit of an attending priest.

Claddagh ring: The traditional Irish design symbolically sums up the essence of marriage: Two hands of friendship clasp a heart for love, above which rests a crown for eternal honor and loyalty.

Mead: The ancient, potent brew fermented from honey is served to the wedding couple, with the intention of increasing her fertility and his virility.

Salt and oatmeal: Bride and groom together take three bites each of these down-to-earth, hearth-and-home foods to ward off the evil eye at the beginning of their wedding banquet.

Kidnapping the bride: The wedding party traditionally ends with the groom picking up and carrying off his bride, a playful reference to the ancient practice of mead-intoxicated men kidnapping the women they wanted to make their wives (see "The Origins of the Honeymoon," page 77).

HELP WITH LIFE'S LOAD
♥♥♥

If you had to carry a load and use your hands at the same time, it would be possible only if the load were strapped on your back: and this is marriage. I found out that when I married, I suddenly had my hands free. But if you drag that load without marriage, your hands are so full that you can do nothing else.   —*Anna Karenina* (1873–1876), Leo Tolstoy

THE SIX WIVES OF HENRY VIII

♥♥♥

As well as establishing the Church of England and paving the way for England to become a world power, King Henry VIII (1491–1547) gained renown for the six formidable women he married. Here, in sequence, are his brides, and the years of their marriages.

1. **Catherine of Aragon** (1509–1533), Spanish princess, marriage annulled.
2. **Anne Boleyn** (1533–1536), lady-in-waiting to the French queen, gave birth to future Queen Elizabeth I in 1533, beheaded on trumped-up charges of adultery.
3. **Jane Seymour** (1536–1537), lady-in-waiting to Queen Catherine, died two weeks after giving birth to Prince Edward, the future King Edward VI. She was the only one of Henry's wives to be buried with him.
4. **Anne of Cleves** (1540), Dutch royalty, marriage annulled in July, six months after the wedding. The marriage was reportedly never consummated, and Anne lived out her years with the official title of "King's Sister."
5. **Catherine Howard** (1540–1542), Anne Boleyn's first cousin, beheaded on charges of adultery. Henry nicknamed the young queen his "rose without a thorn." She was buried next to her cousin Anne at the Tower of London.
6. **Catherine Parr** (1543–1547), daughter of an English courtier, widowed upon Henry's death. She subsequently married Edward Seymour, brother of Jane Seymour and uncle to King Edward VI.

BRUTES WITHOUT YOU

♥♥♥

O woman! lovely woman! Nature made thee
To temper man: we had been brutes without you.
Angels are painted fair, to look like you;
There's in you all that we believe of heaven,
Amazing brightness, purity, and truth,
Eternal joy, and everlasting love.
—*Venice Preserved* (1682), Thomas Otway

TOP RECENT CHAMPAGNE VINTAGES

▼▼

Looking for sparkling wine to toast the wedding? Only sparklers from the Champagne region of France can truly be called Champagne. The top houses put a date only on wines from superior years, which are then aged for three years before release, a total of four years after the vintage date. Those wines from less-than-stellar harvests are blended as perfectly fine nonvintage Champagne. For a memorable first sip together, watch for the following particular vintages. But also bear in mind that nonvintage Champagnes from top labels can often be outstanding, as can many other sparklers. When in doubt, consult a reputable wine merchant.

Year	Rating
1999	Very Good
1998	Outstanding
1997	Very Good
1996	Outstanding
1995	Outstanding
1993	Very Good
1990	Outstanding
1989	Outstanding
1988	Outstanding
1986	Very Good
1985	A Classic
1982	Outstanding
1979	Outstanding

A SURPRISE, PLEASANT OR UN

▼▼▼

"Pardon me, you are not engaged to any one. When you do become engaged to some one, I, or your father, should his health permit him, will inform you of the fact. An engagement should come on a young girl as a surprise, pleasant or unpleasant, as the case may be. It is hardly a matter that she could be allowed to arrange for herself."

—*The Importance of Being Earnest* (1895), Oscar Wilde

A BRIDAL WREATH

▼▼▼

> For their elder Sister's hair
> Martha does a wreath prepare
> Of bridal rose, ornate and gay:
> To-morrow is the wedding day.
> —"She Is Going" (1830), Charles Lamb

SOME LONG-LASTING CELEBRITY MARRIAGES

▼▼▼

Couples who have put paid to the usual Hollywood marriage clichés:

- ❧ Singer **Dolores Reade Hope** and comedian/actor **Bob Hope** (married from 1934 to 2003, when Bob Hope died)
- ❧ Actress **Ruth Gordon** and playwright/screenwriter **Garson Kanin** (married from 1942 to 1985, when Gordon died; Kanin died in 1999)
- ❧ Actress **Jessica Tandy** and actor **Hume Cronyn** (married from 1942 to 1994, when Tandy died; Cronyn died in 2003)
- ❧ Actress **Lydia Clarke Heston** and actor **Charlton Heston** (married since 1944)
- ❧ Actress **Joanne Woodward** and actor **Paul Newman** (married since 1958)
- ❧ Philanthropist **Camille Hanks Cosby** and comedian **Bill Cosby** (married since 1964)
- ❧ Actress **Julie Andrews** and film director **Blake Edwards** (married since 1969)
- ❧ TV reporter **Maria Shriver** and governor/actor/businessman/ bodybuilder **Arnold Schwarzenegger** (married since 1986)
- ❧ Actress **Rita Wilson** and actor **Tom Hanks** (married since 1988)

THE BLUSHER

▼▼▼

The part of the veil that hangs down over the bride's face is technically called the "blusher." When the moment comes to kiss the bride, the blusher is most efficiently lifted by grasping its lower edge at each corner and lifting it up and over the bride's head.

SOMETHING . . .

▼▼▼

Some possible ways to fulfill the old rhyme for bridal attire, which probably became a custom in Victorian England.

Something old . . . *(symbolizing continued ties with family members)*
- Antique handkerchief
- Bible or other religious items
- Family wedding photo, possibly in a locket
- Heirloom wedding dress or lace from the dress
- Mother's wedding band, worn on the right hand

Something new . . . *(for a hopeful future together)*
- Engagement photo, possibly in a locket
- Gown
- Key to the newlyweds' home
- Shoes
- Stockings

Something borrowed . . . *(for good luck, from a happily married relation)*
- Bible or other religious items
- Bridal veil or tiara
- Dad's or Mom's handkerchief
- Earrings or other jewelry, perhaps from the future mother-in-law
- Petal from the groom's boutonniere, inserted into the bouquet

Something blue . . . *(symbolizing fidelity, purity, and nobility)*
- Ribbon sewn into dress or woven into bouquet
- Garter or other intimate apparel
- Nail polish on one or more toenails
- Sapphire or aquamarine jewelry
- Violets or other blue flowers

And a silver sixpence in her shoe. *(a Scottish custom for good fortune)*
- Any shiny (and comfortable) coin minted in the wedding year
- Coin from the bride's birth year
- Old English sixpence, from a coin dealer

GROOM'S AND BRIDE'S BEST FRIENDS

One fashionable twist on modern weddings is to include a beloved pet in the ceremony. Most often, a pet will serve as ring bearer (with the ring attached to the collar) or as a flower girl.

Meatball, actor/comedian Adam Sandler's bulldog, served as ring bearer at the actor's June 22, 2003, wedding in Malibu to model/actress Jackie Titone. The dog wore his own tuxedo, as well as a *yarmulke*, or skullcap, for the traditional Jewish ceremony. And at the July 3, 2004, wedding of actress Tori Spelling to actor/writer Charlie Shanian, the couple's pug and terrier, Mimi and Leah, dressed respectively in a white veil and a tuxedo for the ceremony.

O HAPPY BRIDESMAID!

O bridesmaid, ere the happy knot was tied,
Thine eyes so wept that they could hardly see;
Thy sister smiled and said, 'No tears for me!
A happy bridesmaid makes a happy bride.'
And then, the couple standing side by side,
Love lighted down between them full of glee,
And over his left shoulder laugh'd at thee,
'O happy bridesmaid, make a happy bride.'
And all at once a pleasant truth I learn'd,
For while the tender service made thee weep,
I loved thee for the tear thou couldst not hide,
And prest thy hand, and knew the press return'd,
And thought, 'My life is sick of single sleep:
O happy bridesmaid, make a happy bride!'
—"The Bridesmaid" (1872), Alfred, Lord Tennyson

WEARING WELL

I . . . chose my wife, as she did her wedding gown, not for a fine glossy surface, but such qualities as would wear well.
—*The Vicar of Wakefield* (1766), Oliver Goldsmith

SOME JAPANESE WEDDING CUSTOMS

♥♥♥

Nakodo: This traditional go-between organizes the initial meeting between bride and groom in an arranged marriage and, however the couple meets, assists in both the *yui-no* and the actual marriage ceremony.

Yui-no: A ceremonial exchange of nine symbolic and propitious engagement gifts (see "Nine Japanese *Yui-No* Gifts," page 111).

San-san-ku-do: Whether marriage vows are exchanged in a Shinto shrine, a Buddhist temple, a Christian church, or a civil wedding hall, the service usually includes the Shinto ceremonial sipping by both bride and groom of rice wine *(sake)*—first small cups, then medium, then large—with each cup being raised to the mouth and sipped three *(san)* times to total the lucky number nine *(ku).*

O juju: These 21 two-colored rosary beads are part of Buddhist weddings, with nine beads each for bride and groom, one for each of their families, and one for the Buddha being joined together on a single string.

The cake: Western-style wedding cake is not customary in Japan. But following a banquet of symbolic foods (see "Japanese Symbolic Wedding Foods," page 15), the act of cutting a multi-tiered, beautifully decorated cake has been adopted. Most of the cake, however, is usually an inedible display, with only the top tier real.

Shugi-bukuro: Guests present gifts of money to the wedding couple in these beautifully decorated envelopes.

Hikidé-mono: These presents are given to the guests upon their departure from the party.

Banzai! The traditional raucous Japanese exclamation for good fortune is called out to bride and groom by friends and family as they depart on their honeymoon.

LOVE BEYOND REASON

♥♥♥

I love him with all the strength of my passionate nature, and this, I think, is proper to my youth and sex. If I ask myself why I love him, I find I do not know, and do not really much care to know; so I suppose that this kind of love is not a product of reasoning and statistics.

—*Extracts from Eve's Diary* (1905), Mark Twain

APACHE WEDDING PRAYER

♥♥♥

Now you will feel no rain,
For each of you will be shelter to the other.
Now you will feel no cold,
For each of you will be warmth to the other.
Now there is no more loneliness,
For each of you will be companion to the other.
Now you are two bodies,
But there is only one life before you.
Go now to your dwelling place
To enter into the days of your togetherness.
And may your days be good and long upon the earth.

IN LIEU OF RICE

♥♥♥

The long-held custom of throwing rice at the newlywed couple as they leave the wedding ceremony or wedding party, symbolizing hopes for a fertile and fortunate future together, is falling by the wayside—for two main reasons. First is the concern that grains of uncooked white rice eaten by birds can expand in their stomachs, killing them. Also, rice grains strewn on a hard-surfaced walkway can become as slippery as ball bearings, creating the possibility that the bridal couple or wedding guests may slip and injure themselves.

In lieu of the usual rice, many wedding couples now give guests birdseed or rolled oats to throw. Both of these options are more easily digestible by birds and less likely to cause slippage.

Another alternative is to pass out among wedding guests tiny decorative vials of bubble soap, complete with little bubble-blowing loops, so that the married couple is sent off in a fairy tale–like cloud of sparkling little spheres. Note, however, that bubble soap can itself cause walkways to become slippery, particularly if the wedding is being held in a rainy month.

Some wedding suppliers even provide tiny paper packages containing live butterflies, which guests at outdoor ceremonies release as the newlyweds walk back up the aisle. Some people, however, may consider this cruel to the butterflies.

RANDOM SUPERSTITIONS: GOOD LUCK

▼▼

- **Bells:** Ringing after the wedding (scares demons away).
- **Beggar:** Approaching the bride on the way to the wedding.
- **Cat, black:** Crossing the bride's path en route to the wedding.
- **Cat, house:** Eating out of the bride's left shoe one week before the wedding.
- **Chimneysweep:** Approaching or kissing the bride on the way to the wedding.
- **Clock:** Exchanging vows when the minute hand is rising from the half-hour to the hour.
- **Coin:** In the bride's shoe.
- **Crying:** By the bride on the wedding day (means no tears in the marriage).
- **Dove:** Seen by the bride en route to the wedding.
- **Earrings:** Worn by the bride at the wedding (foretells eternal happiness).
- **Elephant:** Seen by the bride en route to the wedding.
- **Fee to officiant:** An odd sum, paid by the best man.
- **Foot, right:** First step into the place of worship for the wedding.
- **Gown, wedding:** Bride personally adding the final stitches just before the ceremony.
- **Horseshoe:** Open side up, displayed outside the wedding venue or worn, in miniature, by the bride (wards off the devil).
- **Lamb:** Seen by the bride en route to the wedding.
- **Mirror:** Glanced at by the bride just before leaving her home for the wedding.
- **Noise or cheering:** After the ceremony (scares demons away).
- **Moon, full:** Wedding held at this time (foretells lucky marriage).
- **Moon, waxing:** Wedding held when it is growing in the sky.
- **Pearls:** Bride wearing them (wards off tears).
- **Rain:** Falling on your wedding day.
- **Rocks:** Boiling them in a pot (ensures a sunny wedding day).
- **Rosary beads:** Hanging them out your window (keeps rain away).
- **Shoes:** Father (or groom) gently tapping the bride on the head with them before the wedding ceremony.
- **Spider:** In wedding gown (represents money to come).
- **Sunshine:** Illuminating the altar during the ceremony.

RANDOM SUPERSTITIONS: BAD LUCK

♥♥

- **Candlelight:** Illuminating the bride's vision of herself in a mirror just before the wedding ceremony.
- **Clock:** Exchanging vows when the minute hand is falling from the hour to the half hour.
- **Double wedding:** Bad luck for one of the couples.
- **Dress, guest's:** Any skirts longer than the bride's.
- **Flowers, red and white:** Together in the bridal bouquet (represent blood and bandages).
- **Gown, wedding:** Making your own (for every stitch, bride will shed a tear).
- **Gown, wedding:** Colored yellow (jealousy) or green (envy).
- **Groom:** Seen by the bride before the ceremony.
- **Ground:** Bride stepping on it when entering the church (hence, a red carpet or flower petals covering the aisle).
- **Hat:** Dropped by the groom.
- **Mirror:** Bride taking a second glance after she is fully dressed.
- **Monks (or nuns):** Seeing them en route to the wedding (forebode poverty, chastity, or reliance on charity).
- **Moon:** Wedding held when it is waning (diminishing in size in the sky).
- **Name, last:** Marrying a man whose last name begins with the same letter as the bride's.
- **Name, married:** The bride practicing writing it before the wedding.
- **Ring, engagement:** Taking it off, even briefly, before the wedding.
- **Ring, wedding:** Letting another woman try it on (she will steal the fiancé).
- **Pearls:** Bride wearing them (each pearl is a future tear she will cry).
- **Pig:** Seen by bride en route to the wedding (forebodes a swinish union).
- **Postponement:** Of wedding date (could lead to delayed good fortune).
- **Rehearsal:** Bride walking down the aisle before the actual wedding ceremony.
- **Ring, wedding:** Dropped by the groom or best man.
- **Roses, red:** In the bridal bouquet.
- **Weather, stormy:** On the wedding day (forebodes a stormy marriage)

THE UNITY CANDLE

▼▼

A popular practice that began spreading through Protestant churches in the early 1990s, the unity candle is now found in other Christian denominations as well as in some interfaith, pagan, and even nonreligious nuptials. The symbolic ceremony now movingly concludes more and more weddings.

The modern-day ritual usually begins when the mothers of the bride and groom each light one taper at the altar to begin the wedding ceremony. Then, after vows and rings have been exchanged, the officiant will ask the bride and groom to each take one of the tapers and together light the larger central unity candle. Thus, they symbolically take the lights of their single lives and jointly start a new, larger, brighter flame as a married couple. Some couples then extinguish the tapers, while others leave them lit to signify that they remain individuals while also being committed to married life.

LUNCHEON MENU FOR A BELGIAN ROYAL WEDDING

▼▼

The following food and drinks were served at the 1:30 PM luncheon in the Palace of Brussels after the 10:00 AM civil ceremony in the Brussels Town Hall and the 11:00 AM religious ceremony in the Cathedral of Saints Michael and Gudula, uniting Belgium's Prince Laurent and Miss Claire Coombes on April 12, 2003.

Small Ravioles of Lobster Flavoured with Shellfish
❦
Medallions of Milk-fed Lamb with Chopped Parsley
❦
Spring Vegetables in Bundles
❦
Chocolate Sweet Dainties
❦
Chablis Premier Cru Montée de Tonnerre 2001
❦
Château Haut Breton Larigaudière Margaux 2000
❦
Champagne Abelé

SOME LATIN AMERICAN WEDDING CUSTOMS

♥♥♥

Engraving his and her names: In Brazil, the inside of the groom's wedding band is engraved with the bride's name, hers with his name.

Rings before the wedding: In Argentina and Chile, a bride and groom will customarily exchange their wedding rings in the less formal setting of their engagement party. The rings are worn on the right hands until after they are declared husband and wife, at which time they are switched to the ring fingers on their left hands.

Civil ceremony before religious service: Venezuelan couples are generally married twice: first a civil ceremony, and then a religious ceremony two weeks later. Big parties follow both events.

The missing bride: At some weddings in El Salvador, the wedding ceremony begins without the bride or her family yet in attendance. Seven men are sent from the church to the bride's home, to escort her and her family to the church.

No attendants, just parents: An Argentine bride and her groom do not have a maid or matron of honor, bridesmaids, best man, or groomsmen. Instead, they are escorted down the aisle by their parents, who stand beside them throughout the exchange of vows.

Three candles: During a Colombian wedding ceremony, both the bride and the groom light a single candle. Then, with each lit candle, they together light a third, finally snuffing out the first two, thus signifying the end of their former separate lives and the start of a bright new life together.

Singing vows: During the marriage ceremony, Venezuelan couples will sometimes sing to each other special promises of lifelong fidelity.

Thirteen gold coins: To ensure a prosperous life for the newlyweds, in countries including Venezuela, Panama, and Puerto Rico, the families of bride and groom exchange thirteen gold coins, called *arras*; bride and groom may do the same.

A silver rope: Guatemalan couples literally tie the knot during their ceremony, binding their hands together with a silver rope.

Bridal doll and money: In Puerto Rico and elsewhere, a doll dressed like the bride is displayed on the newlyweds' table at the wedding reception. Guests may pin money to the doll's gown as gifts for the couple.

Sneaking away: Venezuelan newlyweds traditionally sneak away from their wedding party, an act believed to bring them good fortune.

SOME LICENSE WAITING TIMES AND AGES OF CONSENT

♥♥♥

The following list indicates the required length of residency before getting a marriage license, waiting days before the wedding, and minimum age not requiring parental consent.

Location	Residency	Waiting Period	Age
AUSTRALIA	None	1 month plus 1 day	18 years
AUSTRIA	None	None	19 years
BAHAMAS	24 hours	24 hours	18 years
BELIZE	None	1 day (residents)	18 years
		3 days (nonresidents)	
BERMUDA	None	15 days	21 years
BRITISH ISLES			
England	7 days	15 days	18 years
Guernsey	1 month	1 day	18 years
Ireland	14 days	8 days	18 years
Isle of Man	15 days	21 days	18 years
Jersey	3 days	7 days	20 years
Scotland	None	15 days	16 years
Wales	7 days	15 days	18 years
CANADA			
Alberta	None	None	18 years
British Columbia	None	None	19 years
Manitoba	None	24 hours	18 years
New Brunswick	None	None	18 years
Saskatchewan	None	24 hours	18 years
COSTA RICA	None	None	18 years
FIJI None	None		21 years
FRANCE	30 days	10 days	18 years
GERMANY	None	None	18 years
HONG KONG	None	17 days	21 years
ITALY	None	None (nonresidents)	18 years
		2 Sundays (residents)	
LEBANON	None	None	18 years (men)
			17 years (women)
MEXICO	None	2 to 3 days	18 years
NEW ZEALAND	None	3 days	20 years
PHILIPPINES	None	10 days	25 years[1]
SPAIN	None	21 days	18 years
SWEDEN	None	None	18 years

Location	Residency	Waiting Period	Age
UNITED STATES			
Most states	None	None	18 years
Exceptions:			
Alaska	None	3 business days	18 years
Delaware	None	24 hours	18 years
DC	None	5 days	18 years
Florida	None	3 days[2]	18 years
Illinois	None	24 hours	18 years
Iowa	None	3 business days	18 years
Kansas	None	3 days	18 years
Louisiana	None	72 hours[3]	18 years
Maryland	None	48 hours	18 years
Massachusetts	None	3 days[4]	18 years
Michigan	None	3 days[5]	18 years
Minnesota	None	5 days[6]	18 years
Mississippi	None	72 hours[7]	21 years
Missouri	None	3 days[8]	18 years
Nebraska	None	None	19 years
New Hampshire	None	3 days	18 years
New Jersey	None	3 days	18 years
New York	None	24 hours	18 years
Oregon	None	3 days[9]	18 years
Pennsylvania	None	3 days[10]	18 years
South Carolina	None	24 hours[11]	18 years
Texas	None	72 hours[12]	18 years
Washington	None	3 days	18 years
Wisconsin	None	6 days[13]	18 years

1. Those 18 to 21 must have written consent from parent or guardian; those 22 to 25 must have written "parental advice" indicating awareness of intent to marry.
2. Waiting period waived if both applicants have completed Florida's marriage-preparation course within the preceding 12 months.
3. Louisiana residents can have the waiting period waived by judicial order. Non-resident visitors to New Orleans do not require a waiting period.
4. May be waived by court order or, in the case of one of the participants being pregnant or near death, via request of an attending physician or clergyman.
5. County clerk may waive for "good and sufficient cause shown."
6. May be waived by a district judge under "extraordinary" circumstances.
7. Judicial district judge may waive when applicants are over 21.
8. Judge may waive when deemed "advisable" that the couple marry sooner.
9. May be waived in some counties for an additional $10 fee.
10. Request waiver by letter to county registrar, along with $15 extra fee.
11. In some counties only.
12. May be waived for military personnel on active duty.
13. Waivable for a $10 surcharge if one or both parties are from out of state.

TOGETHER AND ALONE

▼▼

Love one another but make not a bond of love:
Let it rather be a moving sea between the shores of your souls.
Fill each other's cup but drink not from one cup.
Give one another of your bread but eat not from the same loaf.
Sing and dance together and be joyous,
but let each one of you be alone,
Even as the strings of a lute are alone
though they quiver with the same music.
Give your hearts, but not into each other's keeping.
For only the hand of Life can contain your hearts.
And stand together, yet not too near together:
For the pillars of the temple stand apart,
And the oak tree and the cypress grow not in each other's shadow.
—*The Prophet* (1926), Kahlil Gibran

THE ARCH OF STEEL

▼▼

The arch of steel is one of the most memorable sights at a military wedding. Formed by an honor guard in full dress uniform, complete with their "steel"—that is, swords for the air force, army, or marines, and sabers for the navy—the arch is formed after the ceremony, either in the foyer of or just outside the venue. The honor guard forms two parallel lines and at the words "draw sword" or "draw saber," they raise their steel to form an arch. The newlyweds kiss just before or just after entering the arch, then pass through, symbolically protected by military strength as they enter their new married life. By custom, the last attendant in the arch gently swats the bride on her behind with the side of his sword.

A CLEVER ACROBAT

▼▼

"I can't marry, myself, but I can understand it. I can't stand on my head, but I can applaud a clever acrobat. My dear sister, I bless your union."
—*The American* (1877), Henry James

RANDOM STATS, PART III: WEDDING COSTS

▼▼

$25,000: Average total cost of traditional wedding in the United States.

$7,360: Average cost of a wedding reception in the United States.

$35,000 to $50,000: Price range of an average wedding in New York City.

$31,800: Average cost of a wedding in the greater New York area.

$18,600: Average cost of a wedding in the Southeastern United States.

$19,300: Average cost of a wedding in the Midwestern United States.

$17,500: Average cost of a wedding in the Western United States.

£12,000: Average cost of a wedding in Great Britain.

£14,000: Average cost of a wedding in London, England.

£175: Average cost of a wedding cake in Great Britain.

$800: Average cost of a wedding gown in the United States.

$147: Average cost of one bridesmaid's dress.

$967: Average cost of wedding flowers in the United States.

27 percent: American weddings in which the bride's parents pay all costs.

272,000: Average cost in Yen of a Japanese wedding (about $2,500).

$200: Cost for two-hour wedding photo site rental at the Richard Nixon Library and Birthplace in Yorba Linda, California.

HERE COMES THE BRIDE!

▼▼

In the opening of the doorway was a shower of fine foliage and flowers, a whiteness of satin and lace, and a sound of a gay voice saying:

'How do I get out?'

A ripple of satisfaction ran through the expectant people. They pressed near to receive her, looking with zest at the stooping blond head with its flower buds, and at the delicate, white, tentative foot that was reaching down to the step of the carriage. There was a sudden foaming rush, and the bride like a sudden surf-rush, floating all white beside her father in the morning shadow of trees, her veil flowing with laughter.

'That's done it!' she said. —*Women in Love* (1920), D. H. Lawrence

WHEN TIME BEGINS

▼▼

Women count time from the marriage feast.

—*Nostromo* (1904), Joseph Conrad

CLASSICAL CEREMONIAL MUSIC

▼▼▼

A wide repertoire of classical music selections has accumulated, ones that are well attuned to the various stages of wedding ceremonies, whether played from recordings or by live musicians. To listen to excerpts of those listed, visit an online music source such as iTunes.

Prelude

Johann Sebastian Bach: "Air on a G String"
from *Orchestral Suite no. 3 in D*
Johann Sebastian Bach: *Brandenburg Concerto no. 1*
Johann Sebastian Bach: "Minuet in G"
Samuel Barber: *Adagio for Strings, Op. 11*
Ludwig van Beethoven: "Für Elise"
Frédéric Chopin: "Nocturne in E Flat, Op. 9, no. 2"
Gabriel Fauré: "Pavane"
George Frideric Handel: *Concerto Grosso in D, Op.3, no. 6* ("Vivace")
George Frideric Handel: "Largo" from *Xerxes*
Joseph Haydn: "Serenade" from *String Quartet, Op. 3, no. 5*
Jules Massenet: "Meditation" from *Thaïs*
Camille Saint-Saëns: "The Swan" from *Carnival of the Animals*
Pyotr Ilyich Tchaikovsky: "Waltz" from *Sleeping Beauty*
Traditional: "Greensleeves"
Antonio Vivaldi: "Autumn" from *The Four Seasons*

❦

Processional

Johann Sebastian Bach: "Jesu, Joy of Man's Desiring"
Johann Sebastian Bach: "Sinfonia" from *Cantata no. 156*
Marc-Antoine Charpentier: "Prelude" from *Te Deum*
George Frideric Handel: "Air" from *Water Music*, Suite no. 1 in F
Jean Joseph Mouret: "Rondeau" from *Suite de Symphonies*
Wolfgang Amadeus Mozart: *Piano Concerto no. 21*
Johann Pachelbel: *Canon in D*
Antonio Vivaldi: "Largo" from *Guitar Concerto in D*, RV 93
Antonio Vivaldi: "Spring" from *The Four Seasons*
Antonio Vivaldi: "Winter" from *The Four Seasons*

❦

Bride's Processional
Jeremiah Clarke: "Trumpet Voluntary"
Edward Elgar: "Salut d'Amour"
George Frideric Handel: "Arrival of the Queen of Sheba" from *Solomon*
Benedetto Marcello: "The Heavens Declare the Glory of God"
Wolfgang Amadeus Mozart: "Wedding March"
from *The Marriage of Figaro*
Modest Mussorgsky: "Promenade" from *Pictures at an Exhibition*
Franz Schubert: "Ave Maria"
Henry Purcell: *Trumpet Tune and Air in D*
Richard Wagner: "Bridal Chorus" from *Lohengrin*
("Here Comes the Bride")

Interlude
Johann Sebastian Bach: "Arioso"
Johannes Brahms: "Waltz in A Flat"
Claude Debussy: "Claire de Lune"
Edvard Grieg: "Hymn" from *Finlandia*
George Frideric Handel: "Minuet" from *Berenice*
George Frideric Handel: "Let the Bright Seraphim"
Ralph Vaughn Williams: "The Call" from *Five Mystical Songs*

Recessional
Johann Sebastian Bach: "Allegro" from *Brandenburg Concerto no. 1*
Ludwig van Beethoven: "Ode to Joy" from *Symphony no. 9*
George Frideric Handel: "Hallelujah Chorus" from *The Messiah*
George Frideric Handel: "Minuet in F" from *Music for the Royal Fireworks*
Felix Mendelssohn: "Wedding March" from *A Midsummer Night's Dream*
William Walton: "A Coronation March"
Charles-Marie Widor: "Toccata" from *Symphony no. 5 for Organ*

RANDOM STATS, PART IV
♥♥

65 percent: Newlywed couples who say they wish they had hired a disc jockey instead of a band for their reception entertainment.
81 percent: Guests who list the entertainment as the aspect of a wedding they most remember.

RANDOM STATS, PART V: AGES AT TIME OF MARRIAGE

▼▼▼

27 years: Average age at first marriage for American brides.

29 years: Average age at first marriage for American grooms.

34.2 years: Median age at remarriage for American women.

37.4 years: Median age at remarriage for American men.

27.4 years: Average age at first marriage for Canadian brides.

29.5 years: Average age at first marriage for Canadian grooms.

25 years: Average age at first marriage for Japanese women.

24.5 years: Average age at first marriage for Vietnamese men.

23.2 years: Average age at first marriage for Vietnamese women.

76 percent: Vietnamese men married by the age of 25 to 29 years.

82 percent: Vietnamese women married by the age of 25 to 29 years.

18 years: Average age at first marriage for Bangladeshi women.

21 years: Average age at first marriage for Bangladeshi men.

20.2 years: Average age at first marriage for Chinese women in the 1970s.

22.7 years: Average age at first marriage for Chinese women in 1993.

24.5 years: Average age at first marriage for Chinese women in 1999.

27.4 years: Average age at first marriage for Dutch women in 1995.

22.6 years: Average age at first marriage for Dutch women in 1975.

27 years: Average age at first marriage for French women in 1997.

29 years: Average age at first marriage for French men in 1997.

4.9 percent: Iranian adolescents who were married, as of 1996.

8.5 percent: Iranian female adolescents who were married, as of 1996.

1.4 percent: Iranian male adolescents who were married, as of 1996.

9.8 percent: Iranian adolescents who were married, as of 1986.

17.3 percent: Iranian female adolescents who were married, as of 1986.

3.4 percent: Iranian male adolescents who were married, as of 1986.

17.5 years: Average age of first marriage in Mongolia.

7 percent: Marriages in Nepal before the age of 10 years.

35 years: Average marriage age for Danish men.

33 years: Average marriage age for Danish women.

26.9 years: Average age at first marriage for Australian women in 2001.

21.1 years: Average age at first marriage for Australian women in 1970.

28.7 years: Average age at first marriage for Australian men in 2001.

23.4 years: Average age at first marriage for Australian men in 1970.

12 to 20 years: Age range for women to marry in the Viking Age (late 8th–11th centuries AD).

A PROPOSAL IN THE SADDLE

♥♥♥

Singing cowboy and cowgirl Roy Rogers and Dale Evans were both on horseback, waiting to make their entrances at a Chicago rodeo late in 1947.

"Are you doing anything on New Year's Eve?" he asked her.

"No," she said, explaining that she had no plans.

"Then let's get married," he suggested.

At that moment, the announcer introduced Roy to the crowd, and without another word from Dale he and his horse, Trigger, went charging into the arena.

Dale's introduction came next. Mounted on Buttermilk, she joined Roy in the spotlight and agreed to marry him.

ELOPING TO GRETNA GREEN

♥♥♥

One of the most romantic wedding venues in the British Isles, the Scottish border town of Gretna Green came to prominence after the passage of England's Marriage Act of 1753, which made it illegal for citizens under 21 to marry without parental permission. In Scotland, however, anyone aged 16 and over could marry of their own free will by exchanging marriage vows in front of witnesses. Thus began the reputation of the village 9½ miles north of the English border as the elopers' destination of choice.

Today, though marriage laws have changed, Gretna Green still treats weddings as a principal industry, offering historic sites and romantic natural venues for ceremonies both planned and off-the-cuff.

TATTOO OR NOT TATTOO?

♥♥♥

With the rising popularity of tattoos today, some brides-to-be face the potentially awkward situation in which the wedding dress of their dreams threatens to reveal skin art inappropriate for the big day. Most tattoos can be concealed by covering them first with a coat of foundation three shades lighter than the bride's skin tone, followed by another coat of makeup that matches the bride's skin. Some entrepreneurs now even market special makeup kits expressly designed to cover a bride's tattoos.

SOME GREEK WEDDING CUSTOMS

▼▼▼

Baby-rolling ceremony: Friends and family bring their babies to the bedroom of the couple-to-be and gently roll their tots back and forth across the mattress, which is scattered with sugar-coated almonds, rose petals, and coins, all to ensure a prosperous and fertile union.

Flamboro: Also to ensure a fruitful marriage, family or friends seek out a tree branch ending in five twigs. To the outermost twig, they tie an apple, and adorn the other twigs with red wool, displaying this "wedding flag" outside the home of the bride for a week before the nuptials.

A lump of sugar: A Greek bride will traditionally tuck a lump of sugar into one of her wedding gloves to ensure a sweet married life.

Wedding parade: The *flamboro* is carried to the groom's home, and then leads the groom back to the bride's home, where her mother welcomes and blesses the future son-in-law with wine, a ring-shaped cookie, and an herbal boutonniere. Bride and groom continue to the church.

Betrothal ceremony: In the first part of the Greek Orthodox wedding service, the best man, the *koumbaros*, holds the wedding rings over the heads of the bride and groom and blesses them three times for the Holy Trinity. Rings are exchanged—three times, of course.

Stephana: Special marital crowns linked by a white ribbon are placed upon the heads of bride and groom and switched back and forth three times. Then the couple walks around the altar three times as prayers are repeated to seal their union. Bride and groom then circle the altar three times while guests shower them with rice or sugared almonds.

Money dance: During the first dance at the party, guests traditionally pin or tape money to the clothing of both the bride and the groom.

PROJECTING WEDDINGS

▼▼▼

Mrs. Jennings was a widow with an ample jointure. She had only two daughters, both of whom she had lived to see respectably married, and she had now, therefore, nothing to do but to marry all the rest of the world. In the promotion of this object she was zealously active, as far as her ability reached; and missed no opportunity of projecting weddings among all the young people of her acquaintance.

—*Sense and Sensibility* (1811), Jane Austen

FOUR-COURSE DINNER MENU FOR A NORWEGIAN ROYAL WEDDING

▼▼

The following menu was served to some 400 guests assembled in the Royal Palace in Oslo following the August 25, 2001, wedding of Mette-Marit Tjessem Hoiby and Crown Prince Haakon.

Mussels Kilpatrick or Oysters Mornay
❧

Fried Filet of Perch or Pike with Cauliflower Puree
❧

Filet of Lamb with Thyme Sauce
❧

Parfait with Mousse of Berries

THIRTEEN POSSIBLY INAPPROPRIATE FIRST-DANCE SONGS

▼▼

The choices some couples make for their first dance song can be astonishing. Hearsay, imagination, and in one case eyewitness experience, are the sources for the following examples.

Title	Artist
Band of Gold	Freda Payne
Bang Bang	Sonny and Cher
The Good, the Bad, and the Ugly [*]	Ennio Morricone
I Will Survive	Gloria Gaynor
Love the One You're With	Crosby, Stills, Nash, and Young
Lying Eyes	The Eagles
Roxanne	The Police
Ruby	Kenny Rogers
Stop Draggin' My Heart Around	Stevie Nicks and Tom Petty
Wedding Bell Blues	Laura Nyro or The 5th Dimension
White Trash Wedding	Dixie Chicks
White Wedding	Billy Idol
Your Cheatin' Heart	Hank Williams

[*] This instrumental appeared as a couple's requested first-dance tune on a song list for a 1969 wedding at Knollwood Country Club in Granada Hills, California .

A HINDU WEDDING, STEP-BY-STEP

▼▼

Traditional Hindu weddings are multi-day affairs rich with ritual and celebration. Some highlights:

Misri: This ring ceremony occurs well in advance of the wedding day. It begins with seven married women drawing the sign of Lord Ganeesha in red powder atop a bowl of rock sugar, *misri*. Prayers are said to various gods by the couple and their parents. The fiancés exchange garlands and then gold rings. The groom's parents place a basket of fruit or other gifts on the bride-to-be's lap to welcome her into the family, then feed her family *misri* to confirm the engagement and promise a sweet life for the couple.

Mehndi: At a ladies' afternoon tea the day before the wedding, the bride-to-be is painted on her hands and feet with *mehndi*, henna, in intricate designs meant to strengthen and deepen the bonds with her husband.

Sangeet: This nighttime pre-wedding party for family and friends enlivens the festivities with popular Hindu music, dancing, and food.

Sagri: In the "acquaintance" party, the groom's female relations visit his fiancée with gifts and adorn her with flowers.

Nav-graha puja: In the homes of both families, a priest says prayers to the gods of the "nine planets" to bestow their blessings upon the couple.

Ghari puja: On the eve of the wedding, the priest says prayers in the family homes of the bride and groom. Staples such as wheat, rice, coconut, betel nuts, and spices are included in the prayers, promising prosperity for the couple. Both mothers put on their wedding clothes and walk to the doorways of their homes carrying earthenware pots of water on their heads, and the water is symbolically cut with a knife to ward off evil spirits. Relatives and friends adorn the parents with flowers and money. Meanwhile, both bride and groom put on old clothes that their families and friends jubilantly tear off to symbolize the end of their former single lives.

Swagatam: For this wedding day "welcome" ceremony, the bride's sisters or other female relatives help her dress in her white wedding sari with red and gold embroidery. Then they fetch the groom and bring him back to the bride's home. She greets him at the door and he gently places his right foot atop hers as a sign of the protective support he will give her. The groom enters and his future in-laws bathe his feet in milk and water.

Madhuparka: The groom approaches the altar, where a holy fire glows, and receives gifts from the father of the bride.

Kanya dan: In this "entrusting of the daughter," mantras are chanted as the father of the bride presents his daughter to the groom.

Pani grahan: With his right hand, the groom takes the bride's left hand, accepting her as his wife.

Pratigna karan: The bride leads her husband around the fire as they recite to each other vows of loyalty, love, and fidelity.

Shila arohan: The bride's mother leads her to step upon a stone slab and tells her of the new married life to come.

Laja homa: Holding her hands above the groom's, the bride drops an offering of puffed rice into the fire.

Lawan phere: To legalize their union, bride and groom walk around the fire four times, once each for Hinduism's four human goals of faith, financial stability, procreation, and the soul's liberation. On each revolution, they stop to touch a stone in their path, representing their ability together to overcome life's obstacles.

Sapta padi: A marriage knot is tied between the bride's sari and the groom's scarf, and a thread, over which blessings have been said, is used to tie their right hands together. Facing north, the couple takes "seven steps" symbolizing key aspects of their life together: food, strength, prosperity, happiness, offspring, long life, and partnership. (See "The Seven Sanskrit Wedding Vows," page 102.)

Abhishek: Water is sprinkled as those gathered meditate on the sun and the pole star.

Saubhagya chinya: The groom marks the bride's forehead with *sindoor*, a holy red powder, as a sign that she is his partner, then gives her a black bead necklace to symbolize his love and devotion.

Anna praashana: Together, bride and groom drop food offerings into the fire, then feed each other a bite.

Aashirwaad: The priest and other elders gathered offer final words of blessing and encouragement to the newlyweds.

Datar: Back at the groom's home, the bride passes a handful of *datar*, salt, to her husband and he passes it back to her without a grain falling. They carefully repeat the exchange twice more, before the bride does the same with other members of her husband's family, symbolizing the way she'll blend into and enhance the family, just as salt does with food.

LOVE, WEDDINGS, AND MARRIAGE IN SHAKESPEARE'S PLAYS

♥♥

Romeo and Juliet (1594)
Three words, dear Romeo, and good night indeed.
If that thy bent of love be honourable,
Thy purpose marriage, send me word tomorrow
By one that I'll procure to come to thee,
Where and what time thou wilt perform the rite,
And all my fortunes at thy foot I'll lay,
And follow thee my lord throughout the world.
(Act II, Scene 2)

♥

The Taming of the Shrew (1594)
Would I had given him the best
horse in Padua to begin his wooing that would
thoroughly woo her, wed her and bed her and rid the
house of her!
(Act I, Scene 1)

♥

Two Gentlemen of Verona (1594–1595)
They do not love that do not show their love.
(Act I, Scene 2)

Why, man, she is mine own,
And I as rich in having such a jewel
As twenty seas, if all their sand were pearl,
The water nectar, and the rocks pure gold.
Forgive me that I do not dream on thee,
Because thou see'st me dote upon my love.
(Act II, Scene 4)

Our day of marriage shall be yours;
One feast, one house, one mutual happiness.
(Act V, Scene 4)

♥

Love's Labour's Lost (1594–1595)

By heaven, that thou art fair, is most infallible;
true, that thou art beauteous; truth itself, that
thou art lovely. More fairer than fair, beautiful
than beauteous, truer than truth itself.
(Act IV, Scene 1)

Henceforth my wooing mind shall be expressed
In russet yeas and honest kersey noes:
And to begin, wench,—so god help me, la!—
My love to thee is sound, sans crack or flaw.
(Act V, Scene 2)

❧

A Midsummer Night's **Dream** (1595–1596)

The sealing-day betwixt my love and me,
For everlasting bond of fellowship.
(Act I, Scene 1)

I will wed thee in another key,
With pomp, with triumph and with reveling.
(Act I, Scene 1)

❧

Much Ado About Nothing (1598–1599)

Speak low, if you speak love.
(Act II, Scene 1)

❧

As You Like It (1599–1600)

No sooner met but they looked,
no sooner looked but they loved, no sooner loved but they sighed,
no sooner sighed but they asked one another the reason,
no sooner knew the reason but they sought the remedy:
and in these degrees they have made a pair of stairs to marriage.
(Act V, Scene 2)

They are in the very wrath of love and they will together;
clubs cannot part them.
(Act V, Scene 2)

It was a lover and his lass,
With a hey, and a ho, and a hey nonino,
That o'er the green cornfield did pass,
In the spring time, the only pretty ring time,
When birds do sing, hey ding a ding, ding,
Sweet lovers love the spring.
(Act V, Scene 3)

❧

Twelfth Night (1599–1600)
A contract of eternal bond of love,
Confirm'd by mutual joinder of your hands,
Attested by the holy close of lips,
Strengthen'd by interchangement of your rings;
And all the ceremony of this compact
Seal'd in my function, by my testimony.
(Act V, Scene 1)

❧

The Tempest (1611–1612)
O heaven, O earth, bear witness to this sound
And crown what I profess with kind event
If I speak true! if hollowly, invert
What best is boded me to mischief! I
Beyond all limit of what else i' the world
Do love, prize, honour you.
(Act III, Scene 2)

Honour, riches, marriage-blessing,
Long continuance, and increasing,
Hourly joys be still upon you!
Juno sings her blessings upon you.
(Act IV, Scene 1)

THE BAHA'I MARRIAGE VOW

♥♥♥

Established in the Middle East during the 19th century as a faith that recognized humanity as one people united by a single God, Baha'i views a wedding as a simple yet profound ceremony of commitment between a man and a woman who have decided to marry and have both received parental consent. Having fixed a date, the couple stands before two witnesses who have been designated by their local Baha'i governing council. Then bride and groom recite, each to the other, a single-sentence vow that, according to their faith, sums up all their spiritual, ethical, and material commitments:

We will all, verily, abide by the will of God.

That said, they are officially wed. They and their families and friends may then celebrate the union following whatever may be dictated by their budget, taste, or the customs of the approximately 235 countries or territories in which the faith is now observed.

OVER THE THRESHOLD

♥♥♥

The groom traditionally carries his bride in his arms over the threshold into their new home together as a way of protecting her from evil spirits that might be lurking in the doorway.

RANDOM STATS, PART VI

♥♥♥

5 years: Average increase in life expectancy for a married person.
56 percent: American adults in 1998 who were married.
24 percent: American adults in 1998 who had never been married.

EVERYDAYNESS

♥♥♥

Things happen to you when you're single. You meet new men, you travel alone, you learn new tricks, you read Trollope, you try sushi, you buy nightgowns, you shave your legs. Then you get married, and the hair grows in. I love the everydayness of marriage.

—*Heartburn* (1983), Nora Ephron

"THERE IS LOVE"

♥▼♥

According to the iTunes Music Store, the following performers are among those who have recorded some version or other of a work entitled "Wedding Song," "A Wedding Song," or "The Wedding Song" in a wide range of musical styles. Only those marked with an * are versions of the very popular "Wedding Song (There Is Love)" written and released in 1971 by Paul Stookey of the legendary folk trio Peter, Paul, and Mary.

- Michael Barrett (new age)
- Marc Black (folk)
- *Captain and Tennille (pop)
- Phyllis Chapell (inspirational/religious)
- Cobalt 2 (new age)
- Colors (folk rock)
- Damita (rhythm and blues)
- Destined (inspirational/religious)
- Bob Dylan (folk rock)
- Richard Friedel (new age)
- Kenny G (jazz)
- Laura Leon (new age)
- Dave Lowe (jazz)
- Martian Acres (folk rock)
- Frank McComb (jazz)
- Ken Medema (inspirational/religious)
- Michel Montecrossa (folk rock)
- Yuko Ohigashi (easy listening)
- *The O'Neill Brothers (new age)
- Tommy D. Now (rock)
- The Psychedelic Furs (rock)
- Tom Rapp (folk)
- Hosea Redditt (inspirational/religious)
- Nathan Roberson (rhythm and blues)
- Smokey Robinson (rhythm and blues)
- Charlie Robison (country)
- *Barbara Rothstein and Gloria Sklerov (new age)
- *Paul Stookey (folk)
- Sweet Sue Terry (new age)
- Tom Wirtanen (folk)

THE SEVEN HUSBANDS (AND EIGHT MARRIAGES) OF LANA TURNER

▼▼

The famed screen goddess once remarked, "A successful man is one who makes more money than a wife can spend. A successful woman is one who can find such a man." Here are the seven men whom Lana Turner married.

1. **Artie Shaw**, bandleader/musician (1940)
2. **Steven Crane**, restaurateur (1942–1943)*
3. **Steven Crane**, restaurateur (1943–1944)
4. **Henry J. "Bob" Topping**, millionaire/socialite (1948–1952)
5. **Lex Barker**, actor (1953–1957)
6. **Fred May**, rancher (1960–1962)
7. **Robert Eaton**, businessman (1965–1969)
8. **Ronald Dante** (real name **Ronald Peller**), nightclub hypnotist (1969–1972)

* Marriage annulled

MARRIAGE'S MOST VALUABLE COMMODITY?

▼▼

The value of children is the greatest of all encouragements to marriage. We cannot, therefore, wonder that the people in North America should generally marry very young. Notwithstanding the great increase occasioned by such early marriages, there is a continual complaint of the scarcity of hands in North America. The demand for labourers, the funds destined for maintaining them increase, it seems, still faster than they can find labourers to employ.

—*The Wealth of Nations* (1776), Adam Smith

THE ORIGINS OF THE HONEYMOON

▼▼

The word "honeymoon" comes from the ancient Norse *hjunottsmanathr*, or "honey month." Originally, the traditional getaway was sweet in little more than name, and the fact that the honey was fermented to make the alcoholic drink known as mead. The Norse term referred to the practice of marauding men who abducted women and then went into hiding, along with plenty of mead, until the young women's families stopped searching.

RECENT MARRIAGE RATES BY COUNTRY

♥ ♥

Following are the number of marriages performed per 1,000 population per year, compiled from national censuses, United Nations studies, and other sources. (*Note:* In most cases these rates are declining annually.)

35.1
U.S. Virgin Islands

19.7
Maldives

14.2
Philippines

12
Syria

10.8
Cyprus

9.2
Mauritius

8.4
Indonesia

8.2
Thailand
United States

7.8
Mongolia

7.7
China
South Korea
Turkey

7.6
Mexico

7.3
Belarus

6.7
Denmark

6.6
Israel

6.4
Greece
Portugal

6.3
Japan

6.2
Russia
Ukraine

6.1
Romania

5.9
Australia

5.6
Netherlands
Norway

5.5
New Zealand
Poland

5.2
Czech Republic
France
Germany

5.1
Cuba
Finland
Ireland
Spain
United Kingdom

4.9
Luxembourg
Switzerland

4.8
Austria
Guatemala
Hungary
Italy
Slovakia

4.6
Chile
Lithuania

4.3
Belgium
Bulgaria

4.2
Argentina

4
Sweden

3.9
Latvia
Slovenia

3.8
Venezuela

3.5
South Africa

2
Serbia
Montenegro

RANDOM STATS, PART VII

♥♥

500,000: Number of "destination" weddings held annually in the United States.

100,000: Number of "destination" weddings held annually in Las Vegas.

25,000: Number of "destination" weddings held annually in Hawaii.

4,000: Number of "destination" weddings held annually in the Bahamas.

5,000: Number of "destination" weddings held annually in Jamaica.

5,100: Number of "destination" weddings held annually in the U.S. Virgin Islands.

9 days: Length of average honeymoon.

46 percent: Honeymooners who stay in a hotel or motel.

35 percent: Honeymooners who stay at a resort.

20 percent: Couples who honeymoon on a boat or ship.

8 percent: Honeymooners who stay at a bed-and-breakfast or inn.

9 percent: Honeymooners who stay somewhere else.

76.2 percent: Honeymoons that involve travel by airplane.

SUCCESS IN REPETITION

A successful marriage requires falling in love many times, always with the same person.

—*The Second Neurotic's Notebook* (1966), Mignon McLaughlin

WEIRD LAWS: COURTSHIP

❤❤

A random compendium of archaic or just plain strange courtship-related laws still on the books. (See also "Weird Laws: Single Life," page 16; "Weird Laws: Weddings," page 125; and "Weird Laws: Married Life," page 166.)

No winking! In **Ottumwa, Iowa**, men are forbidden from winking at women they do not know.

No flirting with eyes! A similar offence in the state of **New York** can lead to a $25 fine for the first offense of eyeballing a woman in public, and the penalty of wearing horse blinkers when out on the street for a subsequent offense.

No flirting with eyes or hands! Neither men nor women may use their eyes or hands to flirt in the city of **San Antonio, Texas**.

No flirting, period! A man and woman caught flirting on the streets of **Little Rock, Arkansas,** may be sentenced to 30 days in jail.

Put down that phone! Women in **Dyersburg, Tennessee,** are prohibited from calling up men to ask them for dates.

No cheap candy gifts! The state of **Idaho** requires that gifts of candy given by a man to his lady friend must weigh at least 50 pounds.

Shave it off! Men sporting moustaches are forbidden from kissing women in the states of **Iowa** and **Illinois** and in the city of **Eureka, Nevada**.

Time that kiss! Kisses are prohibited from lasting more than five minutes in the state of **Iowa**.

Ne baissez pas! In **France**, you cannot kiss on a railway train.

Pipe down! The city of **Kalamazoo, Michigan,** prohibits men from serenading their sweethearts in public.

THE ATTENTIONS OF SUITORS

❤❤

You may be ever so much of a gentleman and a privy councillor, but if you have a daughter you cannot be secure of immunity from that petty bourgeois atmosphere which is so often brought into your house and into your mood by the attentions of suitors, by matchmaking and marriage. . . . Above all, I cannot understand why a creature utterly alien to my habits, my studies, my whole manner of life, completely different from the people I like, should come and see me every day, and every day should dine with me. My wife and my servants mysteriously whisper that he is a suitor, but still I don't understand his presence; it rouses in me the same wonder and perplexity as if they were to set a Zulu beside me at the table. And it seems strange to me, too, that my daughter, whom I am used to thinking of as a child, should love that cravat, those eyes, those soft cheeks.

—"A Dreary Story" (1889), Anton Chekhov

ENGAGED BEFORE THE SECOND COURSE
▼▼▼

British naval commander, Antarctic explorer, and World War I hero Edward Ratcliffe Evans was seated next to his beautiful blonde Norwegian wife-to-be Elsa at a formal dinner party in Oslo.

"Do you like soup?" he asked her, trying awkwardly to make conversation.

"No," she replied.

"Neither do I," he said. "Let's get married."

A TOAST!
▼▼▼

The term "toast" for spoken good wishes addressed by a couple to the bridal couple during their wedding banquet comes from a long-ago French custom of placing a piece of toast at the bottom of a communal wine goblet at any special celebration. The goblet was passed from one guest to the next, each person drinking and offering his or her own kind words, until it ended at the person or persons of honor, who drank the last drops of wine in the goblet before literally receiving, and eating, the toast.

GOLDEN MEMORIES
▼▼▼

The heart of marriage is memories; and if the two of you happen to have the same ones and can savor your reruns, then your marriage is a gift from the gods.

—Bill Cosby (born 1937)

BRING HOME THE BRIDE

▼▼▼

Open the temple gates unto my love,
Open them wide that she may enter in,
And all the postes adorne as doth behove
And all the pillours deck with girlands trim,
For to recyve this Saynt with honour dew,
That commeth in to you.

***

Bring her up to th'high altar, that she may
The sacred ceremonies there partake,
The which do endless matrimony make,
And let the roring Organs loudly play
The praises of the Lord in lively notes,
The whiles with hollow throates
The Choristers the joyous Antheme sing,
That all the woods may answere and their eccho ring.

***

Now al is done; bring home the bride againe,
Bring home the triumph of our victory,
Bring home with you the glory of her gaine,
With joyance bring her and with jollity.
Never had man more joyfull day then this,
Whom heaven would heape with blis.
Make feast therefore now all this live long day,
This day for ever to me holy is.
—*Epithalamion* (1595), Edmund Spenser

SOME KLINGON WEDDING CUSTOMS

▼▼▼

Natives of the warrior planet Klingon, part of the *Star Trek* universe created by the late Gene Rodenberry and the creative team that continued his work, observe marriage rituals far different from those of humans. Witness evidence pieced together from the *Star Trek: Deep Space Nine* episode "You Are Cordially Invited . . . ," in which Lieutenant Commander Worf marries the symbiont host (an organism hosting another long-lived life force) Lieutenant Commander Jadzia Dax; the book *Star Trek:*

Celebrations by Maureen McTigue; and from several Internet accounts of Klingon-style weddings held by devoted *Star Trek* enthusiasts. (See also "Las Vegas Weddings," page 122–123.)

Bride's evaluation by the mistress of the house: A non-Klingon bride is seriously questioned by the mother of the groom or the lead female of the House (family), who quizzes her on the history of the House into which she will be entering. Few brides meet with approval.

Bachelor party: Not an occasion to be thought of as fun in any conventional earthling sense, this event, *Kalhyah*, dedicates itself to six themes: deprivation, bloodletting, pain, sacrifice, anguish, and death.

Battle uniforms: Klingons being warriors, battle uniforms make appropriate wedding attire.

Mock battle: Bride and groom may wage mock warfare with each other using the Klingon sword, *betleH*.

Succinct ceremony and vows: Conducted in the Klingon language, the ceremony quickly draws attention to the fact that Klingons stand alone, surrounded everywhere by enemies; they live lives of battle, but unite to form a great empire. In that spirit, groom and bride commit to each other with simple questions such as "Do you swear to join together with him/her and stand . . . against all who would oppose you?" or "Do you take him/her?"—to which the appropriate terse answer is *Hija'* (Yes), or simple affirmations along the lines of "I take you for my mate."

Dramatic gestures: Symbolic actions affirm the union following the exchange of vows. The officiant might raise a Klingon dagger over the heads of the couple, and both man and woman jointly grasp the dagger, which they and the officiant lower together, at which time the dagger is (carefully) withdrawn to leave the hands joined. Or the couple may jointly yell a triumphant battle cry.

Shouts of congratulation: The officiant, along with those in attendance, may conclude the ceremony by loudly declaring: *yIn!* (Life!), *batlh!* (Honor!), and *Qapla'!* (Success!).

RANDOM STATS, PART VIII
♥♥

20 percent: American men who propose on bended knee.

4 percent: American men who ask their future fathers-in-law for their daughters' hands in marriage.

WEDDING CAKE ALTERNATIVES

▼▼▼

Many creative modern brides and grooms are foregoing cake in favor of other favorite sweet non-cake edibles, stacked into a tiered construction resembling a traditional wedding cake. Some options:

- Brownies
- Cheesecakes
- Chocolate-covered strawberries
- Chocolate boxes filled with fresh berries
- Chocolate truffles
- Cookies
- Crème brulées
- Croquembouches
  (miniature French cream puffs covered in crunchy caramel)
- Cupcakes
- Éclairs
- English Trifle (sponge cake, jam, fruit, custard, and whipped cream)
- Fresh fruit medley
- Gelatine
- Ice cream cake
- Krispy Kreme or other doughnuts
- Meringue (perhaps filled with whipped cream and fruit to make Pavlova, Australia's and New Zealand's national dessert)
- Rice Krispies Treats
- Tiramisu

GAUCHO WEDDING VOWS

▼▼▼

The gauchos, fiercely independent traditional cowboys of the Pampas, the rugged plains of Argentina, may have the simplest approach to getting wed found in the world today. According to *The Last Cowboys at the End of the World* by Nick Reding, engagement and marriage are accomplished in a simple, swift act as a gaucho approaches the woman he loves and utters a single word:

Vamos. [Let's go.]

SOME HUNGARIAN VILLAGE WEDDING CUSTOMS

▼▼

Bridal procession: In this *naszmenet*, the bride, dressed in an elaborately embroidered dress, parades through town en route to her wedding.

Ransoming the bride: Friends of the groom mock-kidnap the bride as she makes her way to the wedding ceremony. They then negotiate a sizeable ransom that the groom pays to them, which they return to him later that day during or after the wedding party.

Receiving the bride: At the groom's home, his parents traditionally greet the bride with one or more rituals. They might leave a broom propped against the door, with which the bride will sweep the porch to prove her housekeeping prowess. Or they might place an egg on the ground, which she steps on and breaks to ensure her fertility. Honey and a traditional braided cake ensure a sweet married life.

White tent: In the country, wedding ceremonies are traditionally held beneath a giant white tent, symbolic of the occasion's sanctity.

Gifts for groom and bride: The bride gives her groom a set of hand-kerchiefs numbering three or seven, both lucky numbers. The groom, in turn, gives his bride a bag of coins, symbolizing the fact that he will always provide for her.

Soproni wedding soup: A specialty of Sopron in western Hungary, this combination of chicken broth, chicken meat, vegetables, and plump, tender dumplings is often featured at the wedding banquet.

Auctioning bridal dances: At the wedding party, the bride's godfather auctions off dances with the bride, a ritual called the *menyasszonytanc*. The money or household goods guests promise in return for a dance provide a foundation for the newlyweds' life together.

THE BEST IS YET TO BE

▼▼

Grow old along with me!
The best is yet to be,
The last of life, for which the first was made:
Our times are in His hand
Who saith "A whole I planned,
Youth shows but half; trust God: see all, nor be afraid!"
—"Rabbi Ben Ezra" (1864), Robert Browning

A BUFFET DINNER FOR AN ENGLISH ROYAL WEDDING

❤❤❤❤❤❤❤❤❤❤❤❤❤❤❤❤❤❤❤❤❤❤❤❤❤❤❤❤❤❤❤❤❤❤❤❤❤❤❤

After tray-passed hot and cold canapés, the following self-service buffet dinner, jointly prepared by the Royal Kitchens and London-based caterers Rhubarb Food Design, was offered to 550 guests in the State Apartments at Windsor Castle following the wedding of Miss Sophie Rhys-Jones and Prince Edward. The wedding cake was cut before dinner was served.

Coulibiac
(Smoked Haddock, Rice, and Mushrooms in Pastry)
❤

Beef Stroganoff
❤

A Selection of Vegetables and Salads
❤

Fresh Raspberries

FELLOW-FARER TRUE

❤❤❤❤❤❤❤❤❤❤❤❤❤❤❤❤❤❤❤❤❤❤❤❤❤❤❤❤❤❤❤❤❤❤❤❤❤❤❤

Trusty, dusky, vivid, true,
With eyes of gold and bramble-dew,
Steel-true and blade-straight,
The great artificer
Made my mate.

Honour, anger, valour, fire;
A love that life could never tire,
Death quench or evil stir,
The mighty master
Gave to her.

Teacher, tender, comrade, wife,
A fellow-farer true through life,
Heart-whole and soul-free
The august father
Gave to me.
—"My Wife," *Songs of Travel and Other Verses*
(1895), Robert Louis Stevenson

SOME GEMSTONES AND THEIR TRADITIONAL MEANINGS

♥♥♥

Sometimes engagement or wedding rings feature other gemstones in place of or along with diamonds. Most gems have, over time, come to symbolize particular qualities or virtues, or are regarded as conveying certain powers to those who wear them.

Gem	Meaning or Power
Agate	Balance/healing
Amber	Attractiveness/energy
Amethyst	Contentment/creativity/spirituality
Aquamarine	Intuition/spirituality/tranquility
Aventurine	Fortune/healing/leadership
Bloodstone	Courage/wisdom
Carnelian	Energy/inner strength/love
Coral	Well-being
Diamond	Clarity/eternity
Emerald	Love/tranquility
Garnet	Constancy/luck/strength
Jade	Luck/peace/youthfulness/wisdom
Lapis lazuli	Peace/stability
Moonstone	Good fortune/luck/serenity
Mother of pearl	Charity/faith/innocence/sincerity
Onyx	Groundedness/sincerity
Opal	Luck (only if groom's birthstone)
Pearl	Love/positive self-image
Peridot	Calmness/happiness/kindness/protection
Quartz, rose	Calmness/friendship/love/rejuvenation
Quartz, smoky	Communication/fertility/joy/pride
Quartz, white	Clarity/harmony/power
Ruby	Lightheartedness/glory
Sapphire	Chastity/hope
Sardonyx	Happiness
Tiger's eye	Clarity/courage
Topaz	Calmness/fidelity
Tourmaline	Balance/calmness
Turquoise	Harmony/love/wealth

BEST WEATHER MONTHS FOR A WEDDING OR HONEYMOON
♥♥

Here are optimum wedding (and honeymoon) months around the world, based on meteorological readings for the most pleasant weather: average daytime temperatures closest to the high 60s to high 70s F (high 10s to middle 20s C), with minimal precipitation. (Note that places with extreme climates do not fall within these ranges, but their optimum months are still included.)

Africa

Location	Best Months
Accra, Ghana	August
Addis Ababa, Ethiopia	November–January
Brazzaville, Congo	June–August
Cape Town, South Africa	April, September–November
Dakar, Senegal	December–February
Dar Es Salaam, Tanzania	July–September
Johannesburg, South Africa	April–October
Kampala, Uganda	September–December
Khartoum, Sudan	November–February
Nairobi, Kenya	June–October
Lagos, Nigeria	August–September
Port Victoria, Seychelles	June–October
Rabat, Morocco	November–April
Tripoli, Libya	March–April, November–December

Asia

Location	Best Months
Bangkok, Thailand	December–February
Beijing, China	April–May, October
Calcutta, India	December–January
Hong Kong	December–March
Islamabad, Pakistan	December–March
Jakarta, Indonesia	July–September
Kabul, Afghanistan	April, October–November
Katmandu, Nepal	December–February
Manila, Philippines	December–April
New Delhi, India	December–February

Seoul, Korea	April–May, October
Shanghai, China	April, October–November
Taipei, Taiwan	December–January
Tokyo, Japan	April–May, October–November

Australia, New Zealand, and Pacific

Location	Best Months
Adelaide, South Australia	April–May, August–October
Auckland, New Zealand	February–April
Brisbane, Queensland	May–August
Darwin, Northern Territory	June–August
Hobart, Tasmania	December–March
Melbourne, Victoria	April–May, September–November
Perth, Australia	April–May, September–November
Suva, Fiji	June–October
Sydney, New South Wales	April–October
Wellington, New Zealand	November–March

Europe

Location	Best Months
Amsterdam, Holland	May–September
Athens, Greece	April–May
Berlin, Germany	May–June, September
Brussels, Belgium	May–June, August–September
Budapest, Hungary	April–May, September
Copenhagen, Denmark	May–September
Dublin, Ireland	May–September
Edinburgh, Scotland	June–September
Frankfurt, Germany	April–June, September
Geneva, Switzerland	May–June, September
Helsinki, Finland	June–August
Istanbul, Turkey	April–May, October
Lisbon, Portugal	March–May, October–November
London, England	May–September
Madrid, Spain	April–May, October
Moscow, Russia	May–September
Oslo, Norway	May–September

Paris, France	April–June, September–October
Prague, Czech Republic	May–September
Reykjavik, Iceland	July–August
Rome, Italy	April–May, October–November
St. Petersburg, Russia	May–August
Stockholm, Sweden	June–August
Venice, Italy	April–May, October
Vienna, Austria	May–June, September
Warsaw, Poland	May–June, September
Zurich, Switzerland	May–June, September

Middle East

Location	Best Months
Amman, Jordan	March–April, November–December
Baghdad, Iraq	November–December
Bahrain	December–February
Beirut, Lebanon	March–April
Cairo, Egypt	December–March
Damascus, Syria	March–April, November
Jerusalem, Israel	March–April, November
Kuwait City, Kuwait	December–March
Riyadh, Saudi Arabia	December–February
Tehran, Iran	March–April, November
Tel Aviv, Israel	April–June, October–November

North America and Caribbean

Location	Best Months
Acapulco, Mexico	February–March
Anchorage, Alaska	June–July
Atlanta, Georgia	April–May, October
Boston, Massachusetts	May, September–October
Detroit, Michigan	May, September–October
Chicago, Illinois	May, September–October
Dallas, Texas	February–March, November
Denver, Colorado	May–June, September–October
Havana, Cuba	November–March
Honolulu, Hawaii	December–March

Kingston, Jamaica	November–April
Las Vegas, Nevada	February–April, November
Los Angeles, California	March–May, October–November
Mexico City, Mexico	November–March
Miami, Florida	December–February
Minneapolis/St. Paul, Minnesota	May, September–October
Montreal, Quebec	May–September
Nashville, Tennessee	April–May, October
New Orleans, Louisiana	February–March, November
New York, New York	May, October
Philadelphia, Pennsylvania	April–May, October
Phoenix, Arizona	February–March, November–December
Salt Lake City, Utah	April–May, October
San Francisco, California	May–October
San Juan, Puerto Rico	February–April
Santa Fe, New Mexico	April–May, September–October
Seattle, Washington	June–September
Toronto, Ontario	May–June, September
Vancouver, British Columbia	May–June, September
Washington, D.C.	April–May, October

South and Central America

Location	Best Months
Asunción, Paraguay	June–July
Bogotá, Colombia	November–February
Brasilia, Brazil	May–August
Buenos Aires, Argentina	March–May, September–October
Caracas, Venezuela	January–April
Guatemala City, Guatemala	November–February
La Paz, Bolivia	May–August
Lima, Peru	June–October
Managua, Nicaragua	December–February
Montevideo, Uruguay	April–May, September–November
Quito, Ecuador	June–August
Rio de Janeiro, Brazil	June–September
San José, Costa Rica	January–March
San Salvador, El Salvador	January
Santiago, Chile	April, August–October

PENN'S MAXIMS FOR "RIGHT MARRIAGE"

▼▼▼

In his 1682 work, "Some Fruits of Solitude in Reflections and Maxims," William Penn (1644–1718), a devout Quaker convert and the founder of the Pennsylvania colony, set out 556 guidelines for a moral, fulfilled, happy life, covering such subjects as Education, Apparel, Temperance, Murmuring, Friendship, Knowledge, Industry, Government, Patience, Religion, and, in maxims numbers 79 through 87, what he termed "Right Marriage."

79. Never Marry but for Love; but see that thou lov'st what is lovely.
80. If Love be not thy chiefest Motive, thou wilt soon grow weary of a Married State, and stray from thy Promise, to search out thy Pleasures in forbidden Places.
81. Let not Enjoyment lessen, but augment Affection; it being the basest of Passions to like when we have not, what we slight when we possess.
82. It is the difference betwixt Lust and Love, that this is fixt, that volatile. Love grows, Lust wastes by Enjoyment: And the Reason is, that one springs from an Union of Souls, and the other from an Union of Sense.
83. They have Divers Originals, and so are of different Families: That inward and deep, this superficial; this transient, and that permanent.
84. They that Marry for Money cannot have the true Satisfaction of Marriage; the requisite Means being wanting.
85. Men are generally more careful of the Breed of their Horses and Dogs than of their Children.
86. Those must be of the best Sort, for Shape, Strength, Courage and good Conditions: But as for these, their own Posterity, Money shall answer all Things. With such, it makes the Crooked Streight, sets Squint-Eyes Right, cures Madness, covers Folly, changes ill Conditions, mends the Skin, gives a sweet Breath, repairs Honors, makes Young, works Wonders.
87. O how sordid is Man grown! Man, the noblest Creature in the World, as a God on Earth, and the Image of him that made it; thus to mistake Earth for Heaven, and worship Gold for God!

RANDOM STATS, PART IX

▼▼▼

61: Percent of couples who omit the word "obey" from their wedding vows.
83: Percent of brides who take their groom's surname.
15: Percent of weddings held outdoors.

MOST POPULAR WEDDING FLOWERS

❤❤

The flowers are listed in alphabetical order, as preference may vary with location and season. For information on their symbolic meanings, see "Language of Flowers," page 156–158.

- Calla lilies
- Carnations
- Chrysanthemums
- Daisies
- Delphiniums
- Gardenias
- Gerbera daisies
- Hyacinths
- Hydrangeas
- Lilies
- Lilies of the valley
- Orchids
- Peonies
- Roses
- Stephanotis
- Stocks
- Sweet peas
- Tulips

TRANQUILITY, LOVE, AND MERCY

❤❤❤

And among His signs is this, that He created for you mates from among yourselves, that you may dwell in tranquility with them, and He has put love and mercy between your hearts. Verily in that are signs for those who reflect. —The Koran 30:21

A SHORT HISTORY OF MARRIAGE—AND AN ALTERNATE IDEAL

▼▼

Marriage being the destination appointed by society for women, the prospect they are brought up to, and the object which it is intended should be sought by all of them, . . . one might have supposed that everything would have been done to make this condition as eligible to them as possible, that they might have no cause to regret being denied the option of any other. Society, however, both in this, and, at first, in all other cases, has preferred to attain its object by foul rather than fair means. . . .

Originally women were taken by force, or regularly sold by their father to the husband. Until a late period in European history, the father had the power to dispose of his daughter in marriage at his own will and pleasure, without any regard to hers. The Church, indeed, was so far faithful to a better morality as to require a formal "yes" from the woman at the marriage ceremony; but there was nothing to show that the consent was other than compulsory. . . .

After marriage, the man had anciently (but this was anterior to Christianity) the power of life and death over his wife. She could invoke no law against him; he was her sole tribunal and law. For a long time he could repudiate her, but she had no corresponding power in regard to him.

By the old laws of England, the husband was called the lord of the wife; he was literally regarded as her sovereign, inasmuch that the murder of a man by his wife was called treason (petty as distinguished from high treason), and was more cruelly avenged than was usually the case with high treason, for the penalty was burning to death.

***

What marriage may be in the case of two persons of cultivated faculties, identical in opinions and purposes, between whom there exists that best kind of equality, similarity of powers and capacities with reciprocal superiority in them—so that each can enjoy the luxury of looking up to the other, and can have alternately the pleasure of leading and of being led in the path of development—I will not attempt to describe. To those who can conceive it, there is no need; to those who cannot, it would appear the dream of an enthusiast. But I maintain, with the profoundest conviction, that this, and this only, is the ideal of marriage. . . . The moral regeneration of mankind will only really commence, when the most fundamental of the social relations is placed under the rule of equal justice, and when human beings learn to cultivate their strongest sympathy with an equal in rights and in cultivation.

—*The Subjection of Women* (1869), John Stuart Mill

SOME KOREAN WEDDING CUSTOMS

▾▾

Selling the *hahm*: This box, filled with gifts from the groom's family, is paraded through the streets to the bride's home by friends of the groom, their faces disguised with black squid ink. They cry out "*hahm* for sale" and playfully exchange the boxful of presents for food, drink, and money from the bride's family.

Gifting a goose: Since geese mate for life, a groom traditionally presents his wife's mother with one or two live geese. More practical modern Koreans instead substitute a *kirogi*, a beautifully carved wooden goose.

Sharing *jung jong*: During the ceremony, the powerful Korean rice wine *jung jong* is drunk by bride and groom together from cups fashioned from two halves of a gourd specially grown for the occasion by the mother of the bride. After each sips from a cup, the couple pours the wine back and forth and drinks again to symbolize their now-inter-mingled lives.

Throwing dates: Handfuls of the Asian dates known as jujubes are some-times thrown at the bride, usually by the groom's father or parents, to help insure that she will bear many children. The bride will sometimes try to catch the dates in the voluminous folds of the *hwarrot*, or "flower robe," that is traditionally part of her wedding attire.

The noodle banquet: Known in Korean as *kook soo sang*, this elaborate wedding feast has as its centerpiece a soup of beef broth, eggs, vegeta-bles, and wheat noodles. The latter symbolize a long, happy life together.

THE HONEYMOON PHASE

▾▾

As for the bride, she was now in her honeymoon, and so passionately fond of her new husband that he never appeared to her to be in the wrong; and his displeasure against any person was a sufficient reason for her dislike to the same.

—*The History of Tom Jones, A Foundling* (1749), Henry Fielding

RANDOM STATS, PART X: CELEBRITY WEDDINGS

♥♥

$4 million: Cost of the December 6, 2003, wedding at The Lodge at Rancho Mirage in Palm Springs, California, for television *Bachelorette* Trista Rehn and fireman groom Ryan Sutter.

$3 million: Cost of the December 22, 2000, wedding at Scotland's Skibo Castle of singer Madonna and director Guy Ritchie.

$2.5 million: Cost of the November 18, 2000, wedding at the Plaza Hotel, New York, of actress Catherine Zeta-Jones and actor Michael Douglas.

$2 million: Cost of the January 5, 2000, renewal-of-vows celebration at Caesars Palace, Las Vegas, for singer Celine Dion and manager Rene Angelil.

$2 million: Cost of the October 6, 1991, wedding of actress Elizabeth Taylor and construction worker Larry Fortensky at Michael Jackson's Neverland Ranch in Southern California's Santa Ynez Valley.

$2 million: Value of the diamond tiara loaned by jeweler Harry Winston for the 1993 wedding of Marla Maples and Donald Trump.

$1.5 million: Cost of the June 11, 2002, wedding at Castle Leslie, Ireland, of activist/model Heather Mills and musician Paul McCartney.

$1.2 million: Cost of the March 18, 1993, wedding at New York's Plaza Hotel of model Nicole Mitchell and actor/comedian Eddie Murphy.

$1 million: Cost of the April 19, 1997, wedding at a private estate in California of actress Brooke Shields and tennis star Andre Agassi.

$1 million: Cost of the July 29, 2000, wedding in Malibu, California, of actress Jennifer Aniston and actor Brad Pitt .

$500,000: Cost of the December 17, 1994, Montreal wedding of singer Celine Dion and manager Rene Angelil.

$500,000: Cost of the June 12, 1999, wedding in San Francisco of actress Courteney Cox and actor David Arquette.

$500,000: Cost of the March 16, 2002, wedding in New York City of singer/actress Liza Minnelli and producer David Gest.

$250,000: Cost of the December 20, 1993, wedding at New York's Plaza Hotel of tycoon Donald Trump and actress Marla Maples.

$250,000: Cost of Catherine Zeta-Jones's gown by Christian Lacroix, for her 2000 wedding to Michael Douglas.

$250,000: Cost of the wedding banquet for the 1993 wedding of Nicole Mitchell and Eddie Murphy.

$230,000: Cost of the wedding meal for the 1997 wedding of Brooke Shields and Andre Agassi.

$110,000: Cost of Dom Perignon Champagne served at the 1999 wedding of Courteney Cox and David Arquette.

$75,000: Cost of red roses and white lilies decorating the Great Hall of Skibo Castle for Madonna's 2000 wedding to Guy Ritchie.

$60,000: Cost of the reception orchestra for the 2002 wedding of Liza Minnelli and David Gest.

$30,000: Cost of Madonna's wedding gown, designed by Stella McCartney, for her 2000 wedding to Guy Ritchie.

$27,500: Cost of the yellow lace wedding dress worn by Elizabeth Taylor for her 1991 wedding to Larry Fortensky.

$15,000: Cost of the nine-layer cake for the 1993 wedding of Nicole Mitchell and Eddie Murphy.

$10,000: Value of rented goblets gone missing from the 1999 wedding banquet of Spice Girl Victoria Adams and soccer star David Beckham.

$8,500: Cost of the five-tier wedding cake for Catherine Zeta-Jones and Michael Douglas.

$2,500: Cost of the five-tier cake for the 1991 wedding of Elizabeth Taylor and Larry Fortensky.

50,000: Number of flowers used for decoration at the 2000 wedding of Jennifer Aniston and Brad Pitt.

2,000: Austrian crystals in the tiara, which weighed seven pounds, worn by Celine Dion at her 1994 wedding to Rene Angelil.

1,000: Edible flowers on the cake at the October 26, 2002 nuptials of singers Jessica Simpson and Nick Lachey.

900: Guests at the 2002 wedding of Liza Minnelli and David Gest.

300: Guests at the 2002 wedding of Heather Mills and Paul McCartney.

250: Guests at the 1999 wedding of Courteney Cox and David Arquette.

225: Security staffers for the 2000 wedding of Jennifer Aniston and Brad Pitt.

YOU'RE WEDDED!

♥♥♥

This is the biggest, classiest wedding New York has seen in decades!
—Donald Trump on his December 20, 1993, wedding to actress Marla Maples, with whom he split in May 1997, divorcing in 1999

DINNER MENU FOR A DANISH ROYAL WEDDING

♥♥♥

The foods and wines served at the 8:00 PM wedding banquet at Fredenborg Palace following the 4:00 PM wedding of Miss Mary Donaldson and His Royal Highness Prince Frederik of Denmark at Copenhagen Cathedral on May 14, 2004.

Timbale of Shellfish from the Nordic Seas
Sea Urchin Sauce
❦

Roast Venison from the Royal Forests
Rissole Potatoes from Samsø
Peas à la Parisienne
Sauté Mushroom and Morel Sauce
❦

Vol-Au-Vent Perfect Union
White Danish Asparagus and Bornholm Chicken
with a Sprinkling of Apple Cider
❦

White Chocolate Délice
Crown Prince and Crown Princess
❦

La Cigaralle du Prince Consort 2000
Cahors Château de Caïx 1996 En Magnum
❦

Champagne Mercier
Cuvée Frederik and Mary

TRADITIONAL ESKIMO VOWS

♥♥♥

You are my husband/wife.
My feet shall run because of you.
My feet shall dance because of you.
My heart shall beat because of you.
My eyes shall see because of you.
My mind shall think because of you.
And I shall love because of you.

THE DISAPPEARANCE OF THE BRIDE

▼▼

"Anything else?" asked Holmes, yawning.

"Oh, yes; plenty. Then there is another note in the Morning Post to say that the marriage would be an absolutely quiet one, that it would be at St. George's, Hanover Square, that only half a dozen intimate friends would be invited, and that the party would return to the furnished house at Lancaster Gate which has been taken by Mr. Aloysius Doran. Two days later—that is, on Wednesday last—there is a curt announcement that the wedding had taken place, and that the honeymoon would be passed at Lord Backwater's place, near Petersfield. Those are all the notices which appeared before the disappearance of the bride."

"Before the what?" asked Holmes with a start.

"The vanishing of the lady."

"When did she vanish, then?"

"At the wedding breakfast."

"Indeed. This is more interesting than it promised to be; quite dramatic, in fact."

"Yes; it struck me as being a little out of the common."

"They often vanish before the ceremony, and occasionally during the honeymoon; but I cannot call to mind anything quite so prompt as this. Pray let me have the details."

—"The Adventure of the Noble Bachelor" in *The Adventures of Sherlock Holmes*
(1891), Sir Arthur Conan Doyle

A WOMAN'S PLACE

▼▼

In northeastern India's Meghalaya state, the Khasi tribe, which has the nation's highest literacy rate, is a matrilineal society in which grooms are expected to move in with the bride's parents after marriage. A husband's most important role is to help his wife produce children, especially highly prized daughters, and all offspring take their mother's family name. The youngest daughter inherits all family property. Khasi women make all major decisions in the largely agricultural society.

THE SEVEN SANSKRIT WEDDING VOWS

❤❤

Recited at a Hindu wedding, with each vow repeated by the bride and groom in unison as they perform the *sapta padi* (seven steps) portion of the ceremony. (See "A Hindu Wedding Step-by-Step," page 70–71.)

- ❦ Share the responsibilities of home.
- ❦ Fill each other's heart with strength and courage.
- ❦ Prosper together and share with each other our worldly goods.
- ❦ Fill each other's heart with love, peace, joy, and spirituality.
- ❦ Share the blessing of loving children.
- ❦ Strive for and achieve self-restraint and long lives.
- ❦ Be each other's best friend and partner in eternity.

BRIDES BY THE MONTH

❤❤

English folk wisdom holds that the month in which a bride marries will determine her character traits as a wife.

January bride: Prudent housekeeper, very good-tempered.
February bride: Affectionate wife, tender mother.
March bride: Frivolous chatterbox, given to quarreling.
April bride: Inconsistent or forceful, but well-meaning.
May bride: Handsome, agreeable, and practical.
June bride: Impetuous and generous.
July bride: Handsome but a trifle quick-tempered.
August bride: Agreeable and practical.
September bride: Discreet, affable, and much liked.
October bride: Pretty, coquettish, and loving but jealous.
November bride: Liberal and kind, but sometimes cold.
December bride: Fond of novelty, entertaining but extravagant.

RANDOM STATS, PART XI

❤❤

71.5 percent: Weddings held in Spain's Basque Country during the summer months of 2003 that were religious ceremonies.
66 percent: Grooms 30 years or older in Spain's Basque Country in 2003.

OH PROMISE ME!

▼▼▼

One of the most popular traditional wedding songs in the English language, "Oh Promise Me!" with words by Clement Scott and music by Reginald De Koven was composed for the Broadway comic opera "Robin Hood" in 1890, and sung by the hero to Maid Marian. Most often today, it is heard in comic form in period comedies or dramas, warbled in a high voice by a soprano of insufficient talent.

> Oh promise me that some day you and I
> Will take our love together to some sky
> Where we can be alone, and faith renew,
> And find the hollows where those flowers grew.
> Those first sweet violets of early spring,
> Which come in whispers, thrill us both, and sing
> Of love unspeakable that is to be;
> Oh promise me! O promise me!
>
> Oh promise me that you will take my hand,
> The most unworthy in this lonely land,
> And let me sit beside you, in your eyes
> Seeing the vision of our paradise,
> Hearing God's message while the organ rolls
> Its mighty music to our very souls;
> No love less perfect than a life with thee,
> O promise me! Oh promise me!

A DOWRY FIT FOR A QUEEN

▼▼▼

"Now tell to King Harold these my words:—I will only agree to be his lawful wife upon the condition that he shall first, for sake of me, put under him the whole of Norway, so that he may bear sway over that kingdom as freely and fully as King Eric over the realm of Sweden, or King Gorm over Denmark; for only then, methinks, can he be called king of a people."

—The Story of the Volsungs (13th century AD), Icelandic saga

SOME CLASSIC TV SITCOM WEDDINGS

♥♥

Many of the following episodes may be found on DVD or video compilations:

The Addams Family, **"Morticia's Romance"** (airdates September 24 and October 1, 1965): Cowardly Gomez Addams (John Astin) works up the courage to dump his betrothed Ophelia Frump for her more macabre sister Morticia (both played by Carolyn Jones) in the sitcom two-parter.

> *"I'm not worthy of you."*
> —Gomez Addams

All in the Family, **"Mike and Gloria's Wedding"** (airdates November 11 and 18, 1972): The two-part flashback episode recalls the crisis over whether a Protestant, Catholic, or civil ceremony should be held for the wedding of Gloria Bunker (Sally Struthers) and Mike Stivic (Rob Reiner).

Bewitched, **"I, Darrin, Take This Witch"** (airdate September 17, 1964): In this pilot episode, adman Darrin Stevens (Dick York) meets Samantha (Elizabeth Montgomery); they fall in love and quickly marry. Only on the honeymoon does he discover she's a witch.

The Bob Newhart Show, **"Carol's Wedding"** (airdate October 18, 1975): Receptionist Carol Kester (Marcia Wallace) falls madly in love on a blind date and then gets married in a hurried ceremony after her travel agent groom Larry Bondurant (Will Mackenzie) arrives late due to his own ticketing error.

The Brady Bunch, **"The Honeymoon"** (airdate September 26, 1969): In this pilot episode, widow Carol Ann Tyler Martin (Florence Henderson) marries widower Mike Brady (Robert Reed) in a ceremony that turns calamitous thanks to Tiger the dog, then winds up with all six of their mutual kids, and housekeeper Alice, joining them on the honeymoon.

Cheers, **"An Old-Fashioned Wedding"** (airdate May 14, 1992): Bartender Woody Boyd (Woody Harrelson) marries longtime girlfriend Kelly Gaines (Jackie Swanson), although barmaid Carla (Rhea Perlman) plots their astral charts and discovers, quite accurately, that they've picked the worst possible day for the wedding.

Designing Women, **"Come On and Marry Me, Bill"** (airdate April 10, 1989): Charlene Frazier (Jean Smart) marries boyfriend Bill Stillfield (Douglas Barr) despite finding him handcuffed (innocently) to his bachelor party entertainment, then being handcuffed to both of them herself.

The Dick Van Dyke Show, **"The Attempted Marriage"** (airdate November 4, 1967): In a flashback episode, soldier Rob Petrie (Dick Van Dyke) proposes to sweetheart Laura Meehan (Mary Tyler Moore); then a series of calamities keep him from the altar.

Frasier, **"The Ring Cycle"** (airdate September 24, 2002): Daphne Moon (Jane Leeves) and Niles Crane (David Hyde Pierce) elope to Reno, Nevada, then elaborately conceal the fact that they have married from family and friends who are anticipating the wedding.

> *"By the power vested in me by the state of Nevada, county of Washoe and the all-new Lucky 7 Resort and Casino, I now pronounce you husband and wife. Good luck!"* —Officiant at Daphne and Niles's wedding

Frasier, **"Good Night Seattle, Parts 1 and 2"** (airdate May 13, 2004): Against the backdrop of his daughter-in-law Daphne (Jane Leeves) and son Niles (David Hyde Pierce) about to have their first child, Martin Crane (John Mahoney) weds Ronee Lawrence (Wendy Malick) under chaotic circumstances in this series finale.

Friends, **"The One with Ross's Wedding"** (airdate May 7, 1998): In this special hour-long episode, Ross Geller (David Schwimmer) weds Emily (Helen Baxendale) in London, while Rachel Green (Jennifer Aniston), back home in New York, realizes she loves Ross and hurries to London, where Ross accidentally says her name during the wedding vows. Meanwhile, Monica Geller (Courteney Cox Arquette) and Chandler Bing (Matthew Perry) have an unexpected tryst, which ultimately leads to . . .

Friends, **"The One with Monica and Chandler's Wedding, Parts 1 and 2"** (airdate May 17, 2001): In this two-part sweeps special, Chandler Bing (Matthew Perry) freaks out over the thought of getting married and is finally coaxed back to reality by his brother-in-law-to-be Ross (David Schwimmer) and friend Phoebe Buffay (Lisa Kudrow) in time to make it to the altar with Monica Geller (Courteney Cox Arquette).

"I've known Monica and Chandler for a long time,
and I cannot imagine two people more perfect for each other.
And now, as I've left my notes in my dressing room,
we shall proceed to the vows." —Joey Tribbiani

Friends, **"The One with Phoebe's Wedding"** (airdate February 12, 2004):
Joey Tribbiani (Matt LeBlanc) stands in for the father of Phoebe Buffay
(Lisa Kudrow) in her wedding to Mike Hanigan (Paul Rudd), while Ross
Geller (David Schwimmer) and Chandler Bing (Matthew Perry) compete
to be a groomsman.

Get Smart, **"With Love and Twitches"** (airdate November 16, 1968):
Before his wedding with the beautiful Agent 99 (Barbara Feldon),
Maxwell Smart (Don Adams) swallows a top-secret map, and evil attempts
to retrieve it from him threaten to ruin the happy event.

Happy Days, **"RC and LB Forever"** (airdate May 5, 1981): Richie Cun-
ningham (Ron Howard), stationed at a top-secret U.S. Army base in
Greenland, marries longtime girlfriend Lori Beth Allen (Lynda Good-
friend) by proxy, with his pal and best man Fonzie (Henry Winkler) standing in for him during the exchange of vows.

"She looks too good for words. Remember that
bike we saw in the window for $4,000?
Think about that in a white dress, ya know?" —Fonzie

I Dream of Jeannie, **"The Wedding"** (airdate December 2, 1969): Jeannie
the Genie (Barbara Eden) finally marries her astronaut love, Major Tony
Nelson (Larry Hagman), and finds an unusual way to deal with the problem that genies don't show up in photographs.

I Love Lucy, **"The Marriage License"** (airdate April 7, 1952): Ricky (Desi
Arnaz) tricks Lucy (Lucille Ball) into believing their marriage license was
invalid. She insists they do it all over again, from proposal to "I do's,"
exactly as they did the first time.

The Jeffersons, **"The Christmas Wedding"** (airdate December 22, 1976): Son
Lionel Jackson (Damon Evans) finally weds Jenny Willis (Berlinda Tolbert),
over father George's objections to a white Episcopalian minister.

Mad About You, **"Mad About You"** (airdate February 2, 1995): Everything that can possibly go wrong does in the months leading to the wedding of Jamie Stemple (Helen Hunt) and Paul Buchman (Paul Reiser), before Paul comes up with an unconventional idea the day before the scheduled ceremony.

> *"I always knew it was going to be you."*
> —Jamie Stemple

Martin, **"Wedding Bell Blues"** (airdate May 11, 1985): Before their big wedding, Gina Waters (Tisha Campbell) has her wedding dress almost ruined, while Martin Payne (Martin Lawrence) gets trapped in the hotel elevator.

The Mary Tyler Moore Show, **"Ted's Wedding"** (airdate November 18, 1975): Pompous newsman Ted Baxter (Ted Knight) proposes to his sweet girlfriend Georgette Franklin (Georgia Engel) over brunch at Mary's apartment, and she accepts—provided they marry immediately. The freshly ordained Reverend Chaffield (John Ritter) officiates, wearing tennis whites, with Mary as maid of honor and witness.

M*A*S*H, **"Margaret's Marriage"** (airdate March 15, 1977): Nurse Margaret "Hot Lips" Houlihan (Loretta Swit) falls in love with Lieutenant Colonel Donald Penobscott (Beeson Carroll) and marries him, despite a prank played on him by the MASH crew after he gets drunk at his bachelor party.

Mayberry R.F.D., **"Andy Gets Married"** (airdate September 23, 1968): Sheriff Andy Taylor (Andy Griffith) weds longtime ladyfriend Helen Crump (Aneta Corsaut) in a ceremony complicated by the bumblings of his deputy and best man Barney Fife (Don Knotts), who tags along on the honeymoon.

> *"The perfect bridegroom at a wedding should be like the garlic in a spaghetti sauce, present but not too noticeable."* —Sheriff Andy Taylor

Mork and Mindy, **"The Wedding"** (airdate October 15, 1981): Mork (Robin Williams) weds Earth girl Mindy McConnell (Pam Dawber) despite objections and interference from his home planet of Ork, where they ultimately head off for their honeymoon.

Mr. Peepers (airdate May 23, 1954): In this live-broadcast sitcom, shy science teacher Robinson Peepers (Wally Cox) weds sweet school nurse Nancy Remington (Pat Benoit) in a full-blown formal wedding attended by 50 real-life couples on their honeymoons in New York.

Murphy Brown, "Going to the Chapel" (airdates May 14 and 20, 1990): With Murphy (Candice Bergen) as her bridesmaid, reporter Corky Sherwood (Faith Ford) has serious second thoughts, and then an argument with the groom's mother, before her wedding to Will Forrest (Scott Bryce), after which the couple becomes the Sherwood-Forrests.

> *"I was fitted for the dress, I gave the shower. If there is much more to this wedding business, I want to be paid."* —Murphy Brown

My Three Sons, "Wedding Bells" (airdate September 30, 1967): Oldest still-at-home son Robbie Douglas (Don Grady) and the rest of the family oversleep, waking just an hour and three-quarters before his wedding to Katie Miller (Tina Cole).

Petticoat Junction, "With This Dress, I Thee Wed" (airdate November 4, 1967): Betty Jo Bradley (Linda Kaye) has to choose between four dresses—one she bought for herself, a Parisian go-go mini-gown from Cousin Mae, a country hoedown-style dress from Uncle Joe, and her mother's antique gown—for her marriage to Steve Elliott (Mike Minor).

Rhoda, "Rhoda's Wedding" (airdate October 28, 1974): Rhoda Morgenstern (Valerie Harper), in full bridal regalia, winds up catching the New York subway to make it to her wedding to Joe Gerard (David Groh).

> *"You'll meet a wonderful guy, fall in love, decide to get married, and be just as nauseous as I am now."* —Rhoda Morgenstern

Roseanne, "The Wedding" (airdate May 7, 1996): Daughter Darlene Connor (Sara Gilbert) prepares for her beautiful outdoor wedding to David Healy (Johnny Galecki) while her mom, Roseanne (Roseanne Barr), offers advice and her dad, Dan (John Goodman), refuses to speak to her.

Sex and the City, "Don't Ask, Don't Tell" (airdate August 27, 2000): Charlotte York (Kristin Davis) has some reservations as she walks down the aisle to marry her dream man, Dr. Trey MacDougal (Kyle MacLachlan).

"Honey, before you buy the car, you take it for a test drive."
—Samantha Jones (Kim Cattrall)

Sex and the City, **"The Catch"** (airdate August 10, 2003): Charlotte York (Kristin Davis) marries her divorce lawyer, Harry Goldenblatt (Evan Handler), in a traditional Jewish ceremony during which just about everything goes wrong, to joyously liberating effect.

Sex and the City, **"The Ick Factor"** (airdate January 11, 2004): Miranda Hobbes (Cynthia Nixon) finally marries on-again-off-again boyfriend and father of her child Steve Brady (David Eigenberg) in a charming Manhattan community garden setting.

Taxi, **"The Wedding of Latka and Simka"** (airdate March 25, 1983): Cured of multiple-personality disorder by Dr. Joyce Brothers (herself), Latka Gravas (Andy Kaufman) marries girlfriend Simka Davlis (Carol Kane) in a traditional ceremony of their homeland, held in the familiar confines of the Sunshine Cab Company garage.

*"May the stars shine upon you and may God grant you
many children. You are now husband and wife."*
—Priest, to Simka and Latka

A FAIRY TALE
▼▼

Every time I wake up I think it was all a fairy tale—you, the wedding, everything. But I touch you and I see you are here.
—*Shosha* (1978), Isaac Bashevis Singer

RANDOM STATS, PART XII
▼▼

$5,000: Average cost of a honeymoon.
45 percent: Honeymoons taken within the United States by American couples.
22,000: Couples married at Disney World in Orlando, Florida, since 1991.
55 percent: Honeymoons taken abroad by American couples.
60 percent: Honeymoons that involve travel by rental car.

A MOTHER'S DAUGHTER'S MARRIAGE

♥♥♥

In his poem "To H.R.H. Princess Beatrice," Alfred, Lord Tennyson touchingly captures the emotional bonds between a mother and daughter on the daughter's wedding day—in this case, the wedding of Queen Victoria's daughter Beatrice to Prince Henry of Battenburg on July 23, 1885. Tennyson wrote the verse in his capacity as England's poet laureate, a post he held from 1850 to 1890.

> Two Suns of Love make day of human life,
> Which else with all its pains, and griefs, and deaths,
> Were utter darkness—one, the Sun of dawn
> That brightens thro' the Mother's tender eyes,
> And warms the child's awakening world—and one
> The later-rising Sun of spousal Love,
> Which from her household orbit draws the child
> To move in other spheres. The Mother weeps
> At that white funeral of the single life,
> Her maiden daughter's marriage; and her tears
> Are half of pleasure, half of pain—the child
> Is happy—even in leaving her! but thou,
> True daughter, whose all-faithful, filial eyes
> Have seen the loneliness of earthly thrones,
> Wilt neither quit the widow'd Crown, nor let
> This later light of Love have risen in vain,
> But moving thro' the Mother's home, between
> The two that love thee, lead a summer life,
> Sway'd by each Love, and swaying to each Love,
> Like some conjectured planet in mid heaven
> Between two suns, and drawing down from both
> The light and genial warmth of double day.
> —"To H.R.H. Princess Beatrice" (1843), Alfred, Lord Tennyson

MNP

♥♥♥

The shorthand term "MNP" refers to a modest, traditional wedding reception in the style of the American South. It stands for the only menu items: **m**ints, **n**uts, and **p**unch.

NINE JAPANESE YUI-NO GIFTS

▼▼

A key moment leading to a traditional Japanese wedding is the *yui-no,* a betrothal ceremony derived from a verb meaning "to apply." Held on a day deemed propitious by the Japanese almanac, the event is conducted through a go-between. It brings together both bride's and groom's families for an exchange of nine symbolic gifts, in addition to a traditional kimono sash (*obi*) for her, representing virtue, and a man's kimono skirt (*hakama*) for him, a sign of fidelity. The nine gifts:

Naga-noshi: An abalone shell, as an expression of sincerity and generosity.
Moeny: Money, gifts of cash for good fortune.
Katsuo-bushi: Dried bonito, an essential broth ingredient, to symbolize a long-lasting union.
Surume: Dried cuttlefish, representing fertility and a long-enduring marriage.
Konbu: Tangles of dried kelp, in the hopes of many healthy, happy children and grandchildren.
Shiraga: Strong fibers of hemp, whose name also sounds like the Japanese for "white hair," representing marital bonds that are not only sturdy but enduring.
Suehiro: A fan, which when open fully symbolizes a long future full of ever-expanding promise.
Yanagi-daru: A *sake* wine cask made from tender willow (*yui-no*) trees, symbolizing a gentle, obedient marriage.
Mokuroku: A list of all the gifts that have been exchanged, along with the names of the family members who gave them.

A PROPER TIME

▼▼

> Misses! the tale that I relate
> This lesson seems to carry—
> Choose not alone a proper mate,
> But proper time to marry.
> —"Pairing Time Anticipated,"
> William Cowper (1731–1800)

SOME WEDDING MOVIES

▼ ▼

From comedy to tragedy, musical to romance, these films centered on weddings can provide welcome distractions during the tense moments leading up to the big day, or good fun on anniversaries. Look for the films in this arbitrary list on video or DVD. (See also "Some Romantic Movies," page 18–20.)

The Philadelphia Story (1940): Scandal reporter Jimmy Stewart falls for spoiled socialite Katharine Hepburn as her wedding day approaches, while her ex-husband Cary Grant tries to save the day.

> *"Don't you agree that if a man says he loves a girl, he ought to marry her?"*
> —From the screenplay by Donald Ogden Stewart,
> adapted from the stage play by Philip Barry

The Lady Eve (1941): Con artist Barbara Stanwyck leads unwitting millionaire herpetologist Henry Fonda to the altar in this screwball comedy.

> *"When I marry, it's gonna be somebody I've never seen before.*
> *I mean I won't know what he looks like or where he'll come from or*
> *what he'll be. I want him to sort of take me by surprise."*
> —From the screenplay by Preston Sturges,
> based on a story by Monckton Hoffe

Cover Girl (1944): Rita Hayworth plays an overnight Broadway sensation and Gene Kelly her nightclub-owner boyfriend in this singing, dancing, Technicolor extravaganza.

Easy to Wed (1946): In this Technicolor musical comedy, Van Johnson woos playgirl Esther Williams to get her to drop a lawsuit against his employer, and they fall in love.

Father of the Bride (1950): Dad Spencer Tracy is comically swept away by the mayhem of beloved daughter Elizabeth Taylor's ever-more-extravagant wedding.

> *"I would like to say a few words about weddings. I've just been through one."*
> —From the screenplay by Frances Goodrich and Albert Hackett

Royal Wedding (1951): Brother-and-sister-act Fred Astaire and Jane Powell head to London for Princess Elizabeth's wedding and find their own true loves in this classic musical.

Gentlemen Prefer Blondes (1953): Best friends Marilyn Monroe and Jane Russell, two chorines from Little Rock, head for Paris in search of wealthy husbands in this classic musical comedy.

> *"Don't you know that a man being rich is like a girl being pretty?*
> *You wouldn't marry a girl just because she's pretty,*
> *but my goodness, doesn't it help?"*
> —From the screenplay by Charles Lederer,
> based on the book by Anita Loos

High Society (1956): Cole Porter tunes transform 1940's *The Philadelphia Story* (see above) into a delightful musical starring Grace Kelly, Bing Crosby, and Frank Sinatra.

The Sound of Music (1965): Nun-in-training Julie Andrews finds true love with Austrian baron Christopher Plummer in this classic musical, which includes a spectacular wedding scene.

Camelot (1967): Richard Harris as King Arthur weds and then loses Vanessa Redgrave as Guinevere in a stirring screen version of the hit Broadway musical.

The Graduate (1967): College grad Dustin Hoffman gets involved with Anne Bancroft as the notorious Mrs. Robinson, then falls for her daughter Elaine, Katharine Ross, ultimately crashing Elaine's wedding.

The Bride Wore Black (1968): In this Truffaut thriller, just-married Jeanne Moreau's husband is gunned down on the church steps, and she spends the rest of the film tracking down his killers.

Lovers and Other Strangers (1970): A bittersweet comedy about new and old marriages, with Bea Arthur, Bonnie Bedelia, Gig Young, Bob Dishy, Jerry Stiller, a very young Diane Keaton, and an extra named Sylvester Stallone. Also features the Academy Award–winning hit song "For All We Know," popularized by The Carpenters.

The Heartbreak Kid (1972): Newlywed Charles Grodin breaks wife Jeannie Berlin's heart on their honeymoon by falling for pretty, manipulative young blonde Cybill Shepherd in this dark comedy scripted by Neil Simon.

A Wedding (1978): Auteur Robert Altman explores all the darkly comic complications of a big family wedding, with the help of Mia Farrow, Carol Burnett, Desi Arnaz Jr., Geraldine Chaplin, and many others.

Moonstruck (1987): Widowed bookkeeper Cher agrees to marry dull nice guy Danny Aiello, then falls madly in love with his passionate baker brother Nicolas Cage.

> *"Love don't make things nice—it ruins everything. It breaks your heart.*
> *It makes things a mess. We aren't here to make things perfect.*
> *The snowflakes are perfect. The stars are perfect. Not us. Not us!"*
> —From the screenplay by John Patrick Shanley

Father of the Bride (1991): Steve Martin takes on the title role, Diane Keaton plays his wife, Kimberly Williams is the daughter, and Martin Short is an outrageous wedding planner in this update of the 1950 classic.

> *"I used to think a wedding was a simple affair. Boy and girl meet,*
> *they fall in love, he buys a ring, she buys a dress, they say I do. I was wrong.*
> *That's getting married. A wedding is an entirely different proposition."*
> —From the screenplay by Nancy Meyers and Charles Shyer,
> based on the 1950 screenplay by Frances Goodrich and Albert Hackett

The Wedding Banquet (1993): Traditional and modern, Chinese and American cultures clash in a bilingual comedy about a sham wedding from acclaimed director Ang Lee.

Four Weddings and a Funeral (1994): Hugh Grant and Andie McDowell stumble their way toward the altar in this touching comedy set in present-day England.

> *"You're saying marriage is just a way of getting*
> *out of an embarrassing pause in conversation."*
> —From the screenplay by Richard Curtis

Muriel's Wedding (1995): The offbeat Aussie comedy introduces Toni Colette as the hapless title character, who's deliriously obsessed with getting married and with the music of ABBA.

Sense and Sensibility (1995): Emma Thompson, Kate Winslet, and Hugh Grant, along with director Ang Lee, bring to life Jane Austen's tale of manners and marriage in 19th century England.

> *"My heart is, and always will be, yours."*
> —From the screenplay by Emma Thompson,
> based on the novel by Jane Austen

My Best Friend's Wedding (1997): Julia Roberts sets out to sabotage the wedding of best friend and true love Dermot Mulroney to charming fiancée Cameron Diaz.

The Wedding Singer (1998): Always the entertainment but never the groom, Adam Sandler finds true love with waitress Drew Barrymore, while both are engaged to less appropriate mates-to-be.

> *"I realize this comes at an inopportune time, but I really*
> *have this gigantic favor to ask of you. Choose me. Marry me.*
> *Let me make you happy. Oh, that sounds like three favors, doesn't it?"*
> —From the screenplay by Ronald Bass

My Big Fat Greek Wedding (2002): Screenwriter/star Nia Vardalos plays a Greek-American who falls for non-Greek dreamboat John Corbett in this warm-hearted comedy.

> *"Nice Greek girls who don't find a husband, work in the family restaurant."*
> —From the screenplay by Nia Vardalos, adapted from her stage play

Monsoon Wedding (2001): The comic, touching trials and tribulations of a large New Delhi family as they prepare for their eldest daughter's wedding following Hindu traditions (see "A Hindu Wedding Step-by-Step," page 70–71).

CERTAIN JEWELS

❤❤❤

'You blushed, and now you are white, Jane: what is that for?'

'Because you gave me a new name—Jane Rochester; and it seems so strange.'

'Yes, Mrs. Rochester,' said he; 'young Mrs. Rochester—Fairfax Rochester's girl-bride.'

'It can never be, sir; it does not sound likely. Human beings never enjoy complete happiness in this world. I was not born for a different destiny to the rest of my species: to imagine such a lot befalling me is a fairy tale—a day-dream.'

'Which I can and will realise. I shall begin to-day. This morning I wrote to my banker in London to send me certain jewels he has in his keeping,—heirlooms for the ladies of Thornfield. In a day or two I hope to pour them into your lap: for every privilege, every attention shall be yours, that I would accord a peer's daughter, if about to marry her.'

'Oh, sir!—never rain jewels! I don't like to hear them spoken of. Jewels for Jane Eyre sounds unnatural and strange: I would rather not have them.'

'I will myself put the diamond chain round your neck, and the circlet on your forehead,—which it will become: for nature, at least, has stamped her patent of nobility on this brow, Jane; and I will clasp the bracelets on these fine wrists, and load these fairy-tale fingers with rings.'

—*Jane Eyre* (1847), Charlotte Brontë

BEST DAYS OF THE WEEK TO WED

❤❤❤

Each day of the week casts its own particular spell over a wedding, according to the following old English folk rhyme. Sunday, of course, is reserved for prayer.

> **Monday** for wealth,
> **Tuesday** for health,
> **Wednesday** the best day of all.
> **Thursday** for losses,
> **Friday** for crosses,
> **Saturday** no luck at all.
> —English folk rhyme

THE BENCH WHERE IT ALL BEGAN

▼▼

Veteran British Member of Parliament and Labour Party cabinet minister Anthony Wedgewood-Benn, known popularly as Tony Benn and, in his later years, as Lord Stansgate, impetuously proposed to his wife-to-be Caroline nine days after meeting her while a student at Oxford University. He later convinced the town council to let him buy the bench on which the couple sat at that special moment, and it became a cherished garden centerpiece of the Benn family's London home.

DINNER MENU FOR THE FIRST WHITE HOUSE WEDDING

▼▼

Elected as a bachelor, Grover Cleveland, the 22nd and 24th president of the United States, became the first and only U.S. president to be wed in the White House when he married Frances Folsom on June 2, 1886. It was a small event for family and friends—but nonetheless grand, with the residence festooned with flowers and music provided by the U.S. Marine Corps Band, conducted by John Philip Sousa. An informal wedding dinner was served in the family room, with the following menu.

Terrapin

❧

Breast of Spring Chicken

❧

Cold meats

❧

Salad

❧

Fish

❧

Pâté de fois gras

❧

Ice cream molds, bonbons, fruit

SOME WEDDING-RELATED FORTUNE COOKIE FORTUNES

♥ ♥

Traditionally served at the end of Chinese meals, fortune cookies were actually invented in the United States. Rival claims credit either Japanese designer Makoto Hagiwara, who served them at his teahouse at San Francisco's Panama-Pacific Exhibition in 1915, or Los Angeles restaurateur and baker David Jung, who debuted them in that city's Chinatown around 1920. Regardless of their origin, fortune cookies' wide-ranging messages often touch upon topics related to romance, weddings, and marriages. Here is a sampling.

A man's best possession is a sympathetic wife.

❤

A mysterious person enters your life.

❤

Accept the next proposition you hear.

❤

Answer just what your heart prompts you.

❤

Be most affectionate today.

❤

Dizzying changes ahead. Stay calm.

❤

If you would be loved, love and be lovable.

❤

Including others in your life will bring you great happiness.

❤

Love comes singly and leaves accompanied.

❤

Love is not looking at each other
but looking together in same direction.

❤

Now is the time to go ahead and pursue that love interest.

❤

Share your happiness with others today.

❤

Sing and rejoice, for fortune is smiling upon you.

❤

Some pursue happiness. You create it.

❦

That special someone loves to see the light in your eyes.

❦

The one waiting for you when you get home will be your friend for life.

❦

There is a true and sincere friendship between you both.

❦

There is romance in your life.

❦

Union gives strength. Work collaboratively.

❦

You are doomed to be happy.

❦

You form passionate relationships without compromising yourself.

❦

You or a close friend will be married within the year.

❦

You will get together with the one.

❦

You will soon be involved in many gatherings and parties.

❦

You will soon be surrounded by friends and laughter.

❦

You will soon bring joy to someone.

❦

Your dearest wish will come true.

❦

Your future is as boundless as the lofty heaven.

❦

Your future is sweet.

❦

Your future will be happy and productive.

❦

Your life companion is your best investment advisor.

❦

Your love life will be happy and harmonious.

❦

Your romantic life will take a turn for the better.

CLASSIC VOWS FROM THE BOOK OF COMMON PRAYER

♥ ♥

First introduced in England in 1549 and revised repeatedly down through the centuries, the Anglican church's Book of Common Prayer is the source of the most often heard wedding vows in the English language. Here are some excerpts from the 1662 edition.

Dearly beloved, we are gathered together here in the sight of God, and in the face of this congregation, to join together this Man and this Woman in holy Matrimony; which is an honourable estate, instituted of God in the time of man's innocency, signifying unto us the mystical union that is betwixt Christ and his Church; which holy estate Christ adorned and beautified with his presence, and first miracle that he wrought, in Cana of Galilee; and is commended of Saint Paul to be honourable among all men: and therefore is not by any to be enterprised, nor taken in hand, unadvisedly, lightly, or wantonly, to satisfy men's carnal lusts and appetites, like brute beasts that have no understanding; but reverently, discreetly, advisedly, soberly, and in the fear of God; duly considering the causes for which Matrimony was ordained.

***

Into which holy estate these two persons present come now to be joined. Therefore if any man can shew any just cause, why they may not lawfully be joined together, let him now speak, or else hereafter for ever hold his peace.

***

I require and charge you both, as ye will answer at the dreadful day of judgement when the secrets of all hearts shall be disclosed, that if either of you know any impediment, why ye may not be lawfully joined together in Matrimony, ye do now confess it. For be ye well assured, that so many as are coupled together otherwise than God's Word doth allow are not joined together by God; neither is their Matrimony lawful.

***

Wilt thou have this woman to thy wedded wife, to live together after God's ordinance in the holy estate of Matrimony? Wilt thou love her, comfort her, honour, and keep her in sickness and in health; and, forsaking all other, keep thee only unto her, so long as ye both shall live?

***

Wilt thou have this man to thy wedded husband, to live together after God's ordinance in the holy estate of Matrimony? Wilt thou obey him, and serve him, love, honour, and keep him in sickness and in health; and, forsaking all other, keep thee only unto him, so long as ye both shall live?

***

I take thee to my wedded wife, to have and to hold from this day forward, for better for worse, for richer for poorer, in sickness and in health, to love and to cherish, till death us do part, according to God's holy ordinance; and thereto I plight thee my troth.

***

I take thee to my wedded husband, to have and to hold from this day forward, for better for worse, for richer for poorer, in sickness and in health, to love, cherish, and to obey, till death us do part, according to God's holy ordinance; and thereto I give thee my troth.

***

With this ring I thee wed, with my body I thee worship, and with all my worldly goods I thee endow.

***

O eternal God, Creator and Preserver of all mankind, Giver of all spiritual grace, the Author of everlasting life: Send thy blessing upon these thy servants, this man and this woman, whom we bless in thy Name; that, as Isaac and Rebecca lived faithfully together, so these persons may surely perform and keep the vow and covenant betwixt them made, (whereof this Ring given and received is a token and pledge,) and may ever remain in perfect love and peace together, and live according to thy laws; through Jesus Christ our Lord. Amen.

***

Those whom God hath joined together let no man put asunder.

LAS VEGAS WEDDINGS

♥♥♥

No place on earth offers a greater variety of unusual ways to get married. Many companies, organizers, and venues in Las Vegas offer imaginative options, from drive-through weddings complete with "Just Married" bumper stickers to an interstellar ceremony conducted on the bridge of the U.S.S. Enterprise within the Las Vegas Hilton's "Star Trek: The Experience" attraction. But some of the most wide-ranging and varied themed wedding packages are offered by the Viva Las Vegas Wedding Chapel (www.vivalasvegasweddings.com), including the following.

Beach Party: Two surfer dudes carry the bikini-wearing bride on a surfboard to an altar surrounded by sand, palms, and a "party hearty" minister.

Blue Hawaii: An Elvis impersonator sings and officiates in an island-themed setting.

"Bluez Brotherz": Not to be confused, at least in spelling, with the similarly spelled characters created by John Belushi and Dan Aykroyd, two dark-suited, sunglasses-wearing wild men lead the wedding party in a crazy singing, dancing ceremony.

Bond: An impersonator of 007 leads the ceremony after a hot sports car driven by a performer portraying Oddjob delivers the bride and groom.

Camelot: In a Knights of the Round Table setting, either Merlin or King Arthur conducts the ceremony.

Egyptian: In an exotic Ancient Egypt setting, two male slaves carry the bride in on Cleopatra's throne for a ceremony conducted by King Tut.

Gangster: A Godfather-style minister presides in a mafia-style hangout complete with red-checked tablecloths.

Gothic: The chapel becomes a fog-shrouded graveyard as either Count Dracula or the Grim Reaper presides.

Graveyard: The spooky setting features haunting music, two black roses, and a "dead" witness.

Harley: The package includes a two-hour rental of two Harley-Davidson motorcycles.

Intergalactic: In a starship setting, the ceremony is presided over by your choice of familiarly named space-adventure character: Captain James T. Quirk or Mr. Schpock.

Lance Burton Magic: Following an inspiring candlelit chapel ceremony, the newlyweds are whisked off to a performance by renowned magician

Lance Burton, who introduces them to the audience and joins them for a photo to commemorate the event.

Las Vegas: An Elvis impersonator sings and performs the ceremony in a setting aglitter with slots, sequins, and showgirls.

Liberace: Sitting at a grand piano, a top impersonator of the ultimate glitzy Vegas showman plays and sings the couple up and down the aisle and offers his signature candelabra for the lighting of a unity candle.

Phantom: A masked minister officiates in a chapel complete with organ music and theatrical fog.

Pop Music ('50s, '60s, or Disco): Décor of a favorite musical era provides the setting for a ceremony led by impersonators of such favorite real or fictional characters as Donna Summer, John Travolta, or Austin Powers.

Rock-a-Billy: A twanging version of "The Wedding March" accompanies a vow exchange tailor-made for brides and grooms who are more than just a little bit country.

Rock 'n' Roll: The totally rockin' package includes an electric-guitar version of "Here Comes the Bride" and optional-extra impersonators of such stars as Cher, Janis Joplin, Steven Tyler, Jimi Hendrix, Jim Morrison, or Jerry Garcia.

Sigmund and Freud: Not to be confused with the pioneer of psychoanalysis, this ceremony features two comic impersonators of Las Vegas's famed, similarly named magicians extraordinaire, who perform and officiate.

Victorian: The couple experiences a perfectly refined English wedding, complete with Victorian chapel, period music, soloist, punch, and petits fours.

Viva du Cirque: In an awe-inspiring tribute to one of modern Las Vegas's most awe-inspiring forms of entertainment, high-flying acrobats perform while the couple lights a unity candle.

Wassup Pussycat: An expert Tom Jones impersonator performs three songs during the ceremony.

Western: Hay bales and a hitching post complement a ceremony conducted by either an old miner or a Clint Eastwood impersonator.

A BRIDE'S BEST DRESS

♥♥

Until a few centuries ago, most wedding gowns were not white, simply because they were intended for reuse beyond the wedding day as the bride's best special-occasion dress.

RANDOM STATS, PART XIII: WAR BRIDES

♥ ♥

150,000 to 200,000: Estimated number of women who came to the United States from continental Europe between 1944 and 1950 as World War II war brides, that is, foreign nationals who married U.S. servicemen.

50,000 to 100,000: Estimated number of women who came to the United States from Asia between 1944 and 1950 as World War II war brides.

30,000: Estimate of the minimum number of women who came to the United States from Great Britain as World War II war brides.

47,783: Canadian World War II war brides, who married Canadian servicemen serving outside Canada to December 31, 1946.

44,886: Canadian World War II war brides who were British nationals.

1,886: Canadian World War II war brides who were Dutch nationals.

649: Canadian World War II war brides who were Belgian nationals.

190: Canadian World War II war brides who were either Newfoundland or Caribbean nationals (an unusual pairing, granted).

100: Canadian World War II war brides who were French nationals.

26: Canadian World War II war brides who were Italian nationals.

24: Canadian World War II war brides who were Australian nationals.

7: Canadian World War II war brides who were Danish nationals.

6: Canadian World War II war brides who were German nationals.

2: Canadian World War II war brides who were Malaysian nationals.

1: Canadian World War II war brides who came from Algiers, Greece, India, North Africa, Norway, Russia, and South Africa (one from each country).

80 percent: Canadian servicemen who married World War II war brides.

18 percent: Of Canadian servicemen who married World War II war brides, those who served in the Royal Canadian Air Force.

2 percent: Of Canadian servicemen who married World War II war brides, those who served in the navy.

90 percent: Marriages in Pakistan that are arranged.

25 to 50 percent: Estimate range of unions in Japan that began as "arranged" marriages through a matchmaker rather than as "love" marriages.

$500 to $800: Cost of a marriage by proxy (with one or both participants represented by a stand-in) in Mexico.

9,000: Approximate number of marriage licenses in the United States each year that are filed for but not used.

WEIRD LAWS: WEDDINGS

▼▼▼

A random compendium of archaic or just plain strange wedding-related laws still on the books. (See also "Weird Laws: Single Life," page 16; "Weird Laws: Courtship," page 82; and "Weird Laws: Married Life," page 166.)

No drunkenness! It is against the law in the state of **Pennsylvania** for a clergyman to conduct a wedding involving an intoxicated bride or groom.

I dare you! The town of **Lewes, Delaware**, makes marriages entered into on a dare subject to annulment.

Three strikes, you're out (part I)! A woman may not marry the same man more than three times in the state of **Kentucky**.

Don't kiss for that camera! The city of **Boston, Massachusetts,** restricts people from kissing in front of a church, presumably just-married couples included.

Don't sign that register! An unmarried couple that registers in a hotel or motel as man and wife in the state of **North Carolina** is legally recognized as married.

Three strikes, you're out (part II)! Introducing another person as your spouse three times in the state of **Texas** makes you legally married.

You're on thin ice! In **Portland, Oregon**, weddings are restricted from being conducted in skating rinks.

You promised! The law in **South Carolina** requires that the marriage must occur if a man promises to take an unmarried woman as his wife.

Drop your weapons! In the state of **Pennsylvania,** guns, revolvers, cannons, or other explosive devices may not be discharged at a wedding.

TWICE AS NICE?

▼▼▼

Bigamists respect marriage, or they would not go through the highly ceremonial and even ritualistic formality of bigamy.

—*The Man Who Was Thursday* (1908), G. K. Chesterton

BRIDAL ATTIRE

▼▼▼

Can a maid forget her ornaments, or a bride her attire?

—Jeremiah 2:32

ZOROASTRIAN SACRED TEXTS ON WEDDING AND MARRIAGE

▼ ▼

Some excerpts from holy writings of the ancient Persian faith, as still prac-
ticed by the Parsis of India, some followers in Iran, and others, were
reported in "The Marriage Ceremony of the Parsis" (Bombay, 1921) by
Jivanji Jamshedji Modi. Modi abridged that article from a paper he originally delivered in two parts to the Anthropological Society of Bombay
on February 22 and July 26, 1899.

> That place is happy over which a holy man builds a house, with
> fire, cattle, wife, children and good followers.   —The Vendidad

> What a delicious breath marriage sends forth!
> The violet's bed not sweeter! Honest wedlock
> Is like a banqueting house built in a garden,
> On which the spring flowers take delight
> To cast their modest odors.   —The Vendidad

> I say these words to you, marrying brides and bridegrooms!
> Impress them in your mind. May you two enjoy the life of good
> mind by following the laws of religion. Let each one of you
> clothe the other with righteousness. Then assuredly there will
> be a happy life for you.
>
> —The Gathas (Yasna, LIII, 5)

> May the Creator, the Omniscient Lord, grant you a progeny of
> sons and grandsons, plenty of means to provide yourselves,
> heart-ravishing friendship, bodily strength, long life, and an
> existence of 150 years!
>
> —First priestly wedding blessing

> In the presence of this assembly that has met together in [place
> name] on this [date] of the [year] of Emperor Yazdegard of the
> Sasanian dynasty of blessed Iran, say, whether you have agreed
> to take this maiden . . . in marrige for this bridegroom, in accor-
> dance with the rites and rules of the Mazdayasnians, promising
> to pay her 2,000 dirams of pure white silver and two dinars of
> real gold of Nishapore coinage?
>
> —Question asked three times of a witness for the groom's family

Have you and your family with righteous mind, and truthful thoughts, words, and actions, and for the increase of righteousness, agreed to give, forever, this bride in marriage?
>—Question asked three times of a witness for the bride's family

Have you preferred to enter into this contract of marriage up to the end of your life with righteous mind?
>—Question asked three times of both the bride and the groom

I have preferred.
>—Answer delivered three times each by bride and groom

In the name of God, the bestower, the giver, the benevolent!
>—The traditional Zoroastrian benediction, the Tan-Dorosti, which concludes the wedding ceremony

The will of the Lord is the law of righteousness.
The gifts of Vohu-mano to the deeds done in this world for Mazda.
He who relieves the poor makes Ahura king.
>—The faith's most sacred mantra, repeated twice

May there be health and long life, complete Glory giving righteousness! May the visible Yazads (angels) and the invisible Yazads and the seven Amashaspands come to this fair offering.

May this household be happy, may there be blessing! May there be happiness among the people of the religion of Zartosht! We beseech you, Lord, to grant to the present ruler, to all the community, and to all those of the Good Religion, health and fair repute.

May [names] live for a thousand years! Keep them long happy, long healthy, long just! Keep them thus, keep them caring for the deserving! Keep them living and abiding for many years and countless hours! A hundred thousand thousand blessings upon them!
>—Concluding passages of the ceremony

PURE AS GOLD

♥ ♥

Julia, I bring
To thee this Ring.
Made for thy finger fit;
To shew by this,
That our love is
(Or sho'd be) like to it.

Close though it be,
The joynt is free:
So when Love's yoke is on,
It must not gall,
Or fret at all
With hard oppression.

But it must play
Still either way;
And be, too, such a yoke,
As not too wide,
To over-slide;
Or be so strait to choak.

So we, who beare,
The beame, must reare
Our selves to such a height:
As that the stay
Of either may
Create the burden light.

And as this round
Is no where found
To flaw, or else to sever:
So let our love
As endless prove;
And pure as Gold for ever.
—"A Ring Presented to Julia,"
Hesperides (1648), Robert Herrick

SEVEN JEWISH WEDDING BLESSINGS

At the end of a traditional Jewish wedding, the presiding rabbi recites the *shevah berakhot,* seven blessings to sanctify the marriage before God and all those present.

1. Blessed art Thou, O Lord our God, King of the Universe, who brings forth the fruit of the vine.
2. Blessed art Thou, O Lord our God, King of the Universe, creator of everything for your glory.
3. Blessed art Thou, O Lord our God, King of the Universe, creator of humankind.
4. Blessed art Thou, O Lord our God, King of the Universe, who created man in His image, fashioning woman from man as his mate, that together they might perpetuate life. Blessed art Thou, O Lord, creator of humankind.
5. Let the barren city rejoice at the jubilant return of her happy children. Blessed art Thou, O Lord our God, who makes Zion rejoice with her children.
6. Grant perfect joy to these loving friends, as You did in the Garden of Eden so long ago. Blessed art Thou, O Lord our God, who grants joy to groom and bride.
7. Blessed art Thou, O Lord our God, King of the Universe, creator of joy and gladness, groom and bride, mirth and song, delight and rejoicing, love and harmony, peace and friendship. O Lord our God, may there ever be heard in the cities of Judah and in the streets of Jerusalem sounds of joy and celebration, voices of groom and bride, the jubilant voices of those joined in marriage under the bridal canopy, the voices of young people feasting and singing. Blessed art Thou, O Lord, who causes rejoicing for groom and bride.

DRESSED ALIKE

The custom of bridesmaids and groomsmen dressing in fancy attire similar to that of the bride and groom developed centuries ago in Europe as a way to confuse evil spirits or jilted lovers as the bridal couple made their way to and from their marriage ceremony.

RANDOM STATS, PART XIV: ROYAL WEDDINGS

♥♥

12: Number of cakes, the largest nine feet tall, at the November 20, 1947, wedding of Princess (future Queen) Elizabeth to Prince Philip.

150: Guests attending the wedding breakfast of Princess Elizabeth and Prince Philip.

100: Head of cattle served at the feast following the August 27, 1999, wedding in Kampala Cathedral of Miss Sylvia Nagginda Luswata and Ronald Muwenda Mutebi II, the 37th Kabaka (King) of Uganda's Buganda Kingdom, the first royal wedding in that kingdom in over 50 years.

10,000: Guests at the August 27, 1999, wedding feast for the Kabaka of Buganda and his new Nnaabagereka (Queen).

6 months: Length of time it took for over 100 lace makers to prepare the lace for the wedding dress of Queen Victoria in 1840.

£10: Celebratory gift given by Queen Victoria to each of her wedding gown lace makers.

100 meters (109.3 yards): Length of French Chantilly lace used to edge and finish the wedding gown of Miss Mary Donaldson in her wedding on May 14, 2004, to His Royal Highness Crown Prince Frederik of Denmark.

3,000: Approximate number of guests (the entire adult population of Monaco) at a garden party following the civil wedding ceremony of actress Grace Kelly and Prince Rainier on April 18, 1956, the day before their church wedding.

300 yards: Length of Valenciennes lace used—along with 25 yards each of silk taffeta and silk *gros de longer*—in the wedding dress of Grace Kelly in her April 19, 1956, wedding to Prince Rainier.

750,000,000: Estimated number of television viewers worldwide for the July 29, 1981, wedding of Lady Diana Spencer and Prince Charles in St. Paul's Cathedral, London.

16: Guests who attended the June 3, 1937, wedding of the Duke of Windsor, formerly King Edward VIII, to Wallis Simpson at the 16th century Château de Candé in France (see "The Woman I Love," page 140).

405: Combined staff members sent to London to cover Prince Charles and Lady Diana's July 29, 1981, wedding by America's big three television networks (ABC, 180; NBC, 140; CBS, 85).

2,500: Guests attending the July 29, 1981, London wedding of Charles and Diana.

5 months, 23 days: Length of the engagement of Charles and Diana.

60: Participants in the Royal Motorcycle Escort for the procession from the Royal Palace to Brussels Town Hall in the April 12, 2003, wedding of Miss Claire Coombs and Prince Laurent of Belgium.

140 kilograms (308.647 pounds): Weight of the rum-raisin, Viking ship–decorated cake served following the wedding banquet of single mother Mette-Marit Tjessem Hoiby and Norway's Crown Prince Haakon on August 25, 2001, in the Oslo Dome Church.

18 feet: Length of the train of the bridal gown worn by England's Queen Victoria at her wedding on February 10, 1840.

132: Horsemen in the Royal Mounted Escort for the procession from the Cathedral of Saints Michael and Gudula to the Royal Palace in the April 12, 2003, wedding of Miss Claire Coombs and Prince Laurent of Belgium.

3: Number of bridesmaids for Miss Claire Coombs in her April 12, 2003, wedding to Prince Laurent of Belgium.

25 feet: Length of the train on the dress designed by David and Elizabeth Emanuel for Lady Diana Spencer's July 29, 1981, wedding to Prince Charles.

50 pounds: Marzipan used in Charles and Diana's wedding cake.

49 pounds: White icing used in Charles and Diana's cake.

¼ pint: Dark navy rum used in Charles and Diana's cake.

500 pounds, 9 feet: Weight and height of the cake for Princess Elizabeth (now Queen Elizabeth II) and Philip Mountbatten (now the Duke of Edinburgh) at their wedding on November 20, 1947.

800: Guests attending the wedding of Mette-Marit Tjessem Hoiby and Norway's Crown Prince Haakon on August 25, 2001, in the Oslo Dome Church.

18-carat: Size of the sapphire, surrounded by diamonds, on the ring Prince Charles gave to Lady Diana Spencer, the future Princess Diana.

1 million: Number of geraniums, pansies, tulips, and other flowers planted along the procession route and elsewhere in Madrid for the May 22, 2004, wedding of Miss Letizia Ortiz Rocasolano and His Royal Highness Felipe, Crown Prince of Asturias.

BRIDAL BOUQUET STYLES

▼▼

Familiarity with common florist's terms will prepare a bride-to-be for crucial decisions on her wedding bouquet. (See also "Most Popular Wedding Flowers," page 95, and "Language of Flowers," page 156–158.)

Arm spray (sheaf): A bouquet of long-stemmed flowers tied with a ribbon, for the bride to carry along her forearm.

Biedermeier: Concentric circles of small blooms, each circle a different color, arranged in a tightly structured posy for the bride to hold.

Boa: A long length of blossoms and greenery wired together, for the bride to wear draped around her shoulders like a shawl.

Cascade: A full bouquet from which multiple trails of flowers of diminishing size tumble forward.

Composite: What appears to be a single large blossom, made up of individual petals taken from many flowers.

Contemporary: Any of a wide range of creative compositions involving shapes, styles, or blossom combinations of the florist's or bride's own inspiration.

Crescent: Sprays of flowers curve out from either side of a central bouquet.

Nosegay: Also known as a posy, this is the classic small, tightly composed, hand-tied bouquet of blossoms.

Pomander: A small foam ball completely covered in blossoms, hung from the bride's wrist on a ribbon loop.

Specialty or novelty: Any of a variety of creative compositions in which flowers are combined with other objects such as baskets, fans, or prayer books.

Strauss: A natural bouquet of larger, long-stemmed blossoms, usually loosely tied with a ribbon.

Teardrop: A full bouquet from which flowers of diminishing size cascade forward, ending in a point to form an inverted teardrop shape.

A WEIGHTY UNDERTAKING

▼▼

Marriage is such a long-lasting condition that it should not be undertaken lightly, nor without the approval of our closest friends and relations.

—*Heptaméron* (1559), Margaret of Navarre

A BUDDHIST WEDDING PRAYER

♥♥

Today we promise to dedicate ourselves completely to each other, with body, speech, and mind.

In this life, in every situation, in wealth or poverty, in health or sickness, in happiness or difficulty, we will work to help each other perfectly.
The purpose of our relationship will be to attain enlightenment by perfecting our kindness and compassion toward all sentient beings.

—Venerable Lama Thubten Yeshe (1935–1984)

A LOVE BETTER STILL

♥♥

The first phase of married love will pass, it is true, but then there will come a love that is better still. Then there will be the union of souls, they will have everything in common, there will be no secrets between them. And once they have children, the most difficult times will seem to them happy, so long as there is love and courage.

—*Notes from Underground* (1864), Fyodor Dostoyevsky

A PUZZLING PROPOSAL

♥♥

Jigsaw puzzle enthusiasts sometimes make use of their hobby to deliver a marriage proposal. Custom proposal puzzles ranging from small notebook size up to almost two by three feet, and from just a few pieces up to 500 or more, can be easily commissioned from manufacturers (type in the search string "proposal puzzle" on your favorite Internet search engine). The cost ranges from low six to low seven figures, depending on size and intricacy. A puzzle arrives around two weeks from the time of ordering and can also be "rush" ordered for an additional fee.

Solution time can take up to an estimated seven hours. One key way to enhance the puzzle's impact is for the person proposing to omit those few pieces of an elaborate puzzle that actually contain the "Will you marry me?" message, handing them over to the loved one only when their absence is noticed.

WORLD LEADERS ON LOVE AND MARRIAGE

♥♥

I have come to the conclusion never again to think of marrying, and for this reason: I can never be satisfied with anyone who would be blockhead enough to have me.

> —Abraham Lincoln (1809–1865), personal letter, April 1, 1838

❦

My most brilliant achievement was my ability to be able to persuade my wife to marry me. —Sir Winston Churchill (1874–1965)

❦

And one night over dinner as we sat at a table for two, I said, "Let's get married." She deserved a more romantic proposal than that, but—bless her—she put her hand on mine, looked into my eyes, and said, "Let's."

> —Ronald Reagan (1911–2004), *An American Life* (1990)

❦

Really, I do not think it possible for any one in the world to be happier, or as happy as I am. He is an Angel, and his kindness and affection for me is really touching.

> —Queen Victoria (1837–1901), journal entry, February 11, 1840

❦

My life without you is like a year without a spring time which comes to give illumination and heat to the atmosphere saturated by the dark cold breeze of winter.

> —Martin Luther King (1929–1968), letter to Coretta Scott King, July 18, 1952, quoted in *The Autobiography of Martin Luther King* (1998)

❦

The whole purpose of a husband and wife is that when hard times knock at the door you should be able to embrace each other.

> —Nelson Mandela (born 1918)

❦

With the increasing bankruptcy of the rural economy in recent years, the basis for men's domination over women has already been undermined. With the rise of the peasant movement, the women in many places have now begun to organize rural women's associations; the opportunity has come for them to lift up their heads, and the authority of the husband is getting shakier every day.

—Mao Zedong (1893–1976), from *Quotations from Chairman Mao*

❧

The ideal that marriage aims at is that of spiritual union through the physical. The human love that it incarnates is intended to serve as a stepping-stone to divine or universal love.

—Mohandas K. Gandhi (1869–1948)

❧

We were bound first of all by our marriage, but also by our common views on life. —Mikhail Gorbachev (born 1931)

❧

We seem to be bound together with ever-increasing bonds as we've grown older and need each other more. When we are apart for just a day or so, I have the same hollow feeling of loneliness and unassuaged desire as when I was away at sea for a week or more during the first years of our marriage. —Jimmy Carter (born 1924), *The Virtues of Aging* (1998)

❧

Heaven will be no heaven to me if I do not meet my wife there.

—Andrew Jackson (1767–1845)

THE BEST DOWRY

♥♥♥

What matters is not that a married couple should be equal in wealth, but that their minds and manners should be compatible. Integrity and modesty are a girl's best dowry. —Terence (185–159 BC)

MARRIED TO THE MAP

▼▼

A glimpse at any map can reveal surprising geographic resonances with the theme of weddings. Here are some examples from around the English-speaking world, compiled with the invaluable assistance of several atlases plus mapquest.com

Altar Creek, Indiana
Altar Mesa, Arizona
Altar Rock, Massachusetts
Bouquet, New York
Bridal Veil, Oregon
Bride, Tennessee
Bridebridge, Ireland
Brideswell, Ireland
Bridekirk, England
Bridestowe, England
Cake Hill, Wyoming
Cake Mountain, Arizona
Cake Rock, Washington
Diamond, Alabama (also California, Georgia, Iowa,
Illinois, Indiana, Kentucky, Lousiana, Missouri, and Oregon)
Diamond, Ireland
Diamond Creek, Australia
Groom, Texas
Groombridge, England
Honeymoon Bay, Washington
Honeymoon Brook, Maine
Honeymoon Campground, Arizona
Honeymoon Cove, California
Honeymoon Creek, Arkansas (also Georgia,
Idaho, Minnesota, and Montana)
Husband, Pennsylvania
Husbands Bosworth, England
Kissimmee, Florida
Kissimmee, Pennsylvania
Promise, Oregon (also South Dakota and Tennessee)
Proposal Hill, North Dakota
Proposal Rock, Oregon

Ring, Oregon (also Wisconsin)
Ringland, England
Ringmore, England
Ringville, Ireland
Ringway, New Zealand
Romance, Arkansas (also Missouri, Wisconsin, and West Virginia)
Tuxedo, Maryland (also North Carolina and Texas)
Tuxedo Park, Delaware (also New York)
Veilstown, Pennsylvania
Vowchurch, England
Weddington, Arkansas (also North Carolina)
Wedmore, England
Wife Creek, Utah
Wife Lead, New York

MARRIAGE OF TRUE MINDS

♥♥

Let me not to the marriage of true minds
Admit impediments. Love is not love
Which alters when it alteration finds,
Or bends with the remover to remove:
O, no! it is an ever-fixed mark,
That looks on tempests, and is never shaken;
It is the star to every wandering bark,
Whose worth's unknown, although his height be taken.
Love's not Time's fool, though rosy lips and cheeks
Within his bending sickle's compass come;
Love alters not with his brief hours and weeks,
But bears it out even to the edge of doom.
   If this is error, and upon me prov'd,
   I never writ, nor no man ever lov'd.
     —"Sonnet CXVI" (1609), William Shakespeare

RANDOM STATS, PART XV

♥♥

2,327,000: Number of weddings in the United States, in 2001.
7,000: Wedding planners in the United States.

NO HAPPINESS WITHOUT MARRIAGE

▼♥▼

"Nowadays it really seems strange to see a happy man," observes one of the passengers; "one as soon expects to see a white elephant."

"Yes, and whose fault is it?" says Ivan Alexyevitch, stretching his long legs and thrusting out his feet with their very pointed toes. "If you are not happy it's your own fault! Yes, what else do you suppose it is? Man is the creator of his own happiness. If you want to be happy you will be, but you don't want to be! You obstinately turn away from happiness."

"Why, what next! How do you make that out?"

"Very simply. Nature has ordained that at a certain stage in his life man should love. When that time comes you should love like a house on fire, but you won't heed the dictates of nature, you keep waiting for something. What's more, it's laid down by law that the normal man should enter upon matrimony. There's no happiness without marriage. When the propitious moment has come, get married. There's no use in shilly-shallying.

—"A Happy Man" (1886), Anton Chekhov

WHEN GALS DO THE PROPOSIN'

▼♥▼

On November 15, 1937, cartoonist Al Capp launched a modern American tradition in his popular "Li'l Abner" comic strip, set in the Ozark Mountains village of Dogpatch, USA. In that installment, respected townsman Hekzebiah Hawkins, worried that his daughter Sadie remained unmarried, declared Dogpatch's first annual "Sadie Hawkins Day." The celebration's main event was a footrace during which the town's unmarried gals set out in hot pursuit of its bachelors, who were given a very brief head start, winning the right to marry anyone they caught.

Within two years of the initial Sadie Hawkins Day strip, the event was being observed at high school and college campuses nationwide, only slightly modified: Girls got to ask boys to be their dates at a special Dogpatch-themed dance. Though creator Capp bristled at first, he finally consented to let the date of November 13 be observed annually as Sadie Hawkins Day. Capp continued to feature the holiday in his strip each November for four decades, until his death led to the strip's discontinuation. Sadie Hawkins Day, however, lives on.

A PUZZLING TEST OF FIDELITY

▼▼▼

In the first century AD, intricate puzzle rings made up of multiple little pieces that fit together just so when placed on a bride's finger became popular among wealthy Arab traders. When a husband returned home from his travels, an intact ring on his wife's hand offered some reassurance to him that she had remained faithful during his absence.

RANDOM STATS, PART XVI: INTERFAITH MARRIAGES

▼▼▼

100: Dispensations offered by the Catholic Church in 1999 for mixed marriages between Catholics and Muslims in Italy.

12,000: Total registered mixed marriages in Italy as of 2000.

6,000: Total registered mixed marriages in Italy as of 1990.

47 percent: U.S. Jews in interfaith marriages as of 2001.

5,763: Number of Catholics in Pennsylvania who entered interfaith marriages in 2002.

60 percent: Estimated interfaith marriages within the U.S. Greek Orthodox community.

66 percent: Estimated inter-Christian marriages now conducted within U.S. Greek Orthodox churches.

10 percent: Marriages registered by the Reformed Church of Nurnberg, Germany, between 1980 and 1993 in which both participants were members of the church.

80 percent: Marriages registered by the Reformed Church of Nurnberg, Germany, between 1980 and 1993 in which a member of the church married either a Lutheran (40 percent) or a Catholic (40 percent).

1.2 percent: Marriages in Northern Ireland for mixed Protestant-Catholic couples in 1971.

20 percent: Marriages in Down and Connor diocese, Northern Ireland, for mixed Protestant-Catholic couples in 1990.

9 percent: Marriages in Derry diocese, Northern Ireland, for mixed Protestant-Catholic couples in 1990.

4 percent: Marriages in Armagh diocese, Northern Ireland, for mixed Protestant-Catholic couples in 1990.

"THE WOMAN I LOVE"

♥♥

At long last I am able to say a few words of my own. I have never wanted to withhold anything but until now it has not been constitutionally possible for me to speak.

A few hours ago I discharged my last duty as King and Emperor, and now that I have been succeeded by my brother, the Duke of York, my first words must be to declare my allegiance to him. This I do with all my heart.

You all know the reasons which have impelled me to renounce the throne. But I want you to understand that in making up my mind I did not forget the country or the empire, which, as Prince of Wales and lately as King, I have for 25 years tried to serve.

But you must believe me when I tell you that I have found it impossible to carry the heavy burden of responsibility and to discharge my duties as King as I would wish to do without the help and support of the woman I love.

And I want you to know that the decision I have made has been mine and mine alone.

And now, we all have a new King. I wish him and you, his people, happiness and prosperity with all my heart. God bless you all! God save the King!

—Text of the December 11, 1936, radio address to the British people delivered by Edward, the Duke of Windsor, explaining his abdication as King Edward VIII so he could ultimately marry American divorcée Wallis Simpson on June 3, 1937

GOODLY COMPANY

♥♥

O sweeter than the marriage-feast,
'Tis sweeter far to me,
To walk together to the kirk
With a goodly company!—

To walk together to the kirk,
And all together pray,
While each to his great Father bends,
Old men, and babes, and loving friends,
And youths and maidens gay!
—"The Rime of the Ancient Mariner" (1798),
Samuel Taylor Coleridge

SOME WEDDING AND MARRIAGE SUPERLATIVES

▼▼▼

The following facts have been confirmed by various sources, including Guinness World Records.

Largest mass wedding: August 25, 1995, in Seoul, Korea, when 35,000 men and women married in a mass wedding conducted by the Reverend Sun Myung Moon, another 325,000 couples worldwide participated live via satellite.

Biggest underwater wedding ceremony: September 13, 2003, when Toni Wison wed John Santino 10 feet under water off Rainbow Beach at St. Croix, U.S. Virgin Islands, with an underwater officiant and 102 additional diver-guests.

Most couples simultaneously wed underwater: 22 couples, 32.8 feet under water off the shore of Kradan Island, Thailand, on Valentine's Day, 2001.

Most couples wed simultaneously in prison: 120 on June 14, 2000, when inmates of Carandiru Prison in São Paulo, Brazil, wed.

Longest engagement: 67 years, for Mexican nationals Adriana Martinez and Octavio Guillen, who finally wed in June 1969, both at the age of 82.

Most-married man (polygamous): King Mongut of Siam (portrayed in the stage musical and movie *The King and I*), who reputedly had 9,000 wives and concubines.

Most-married man (monogamous): Baptist minister Glynn Wolfe of Blythe, California, who married 22 times.

Most remarried couple: Richard and Carole Roble of New York have been married to each other 56 times since their inaugural ceremony in 1969.

Longest marriage: 86 years, a record shared by Indian cousins Sir Temulji Bhicaji Nariman and Lady Nariman (1853–1940) and Lazarus Rowe and Molly Weber of Greenland, New Hampshire (1743–1829).

Oldest bride: 102-year-old Minnie Munro, wed to 83-year-old Dudley Reid in Point Claire, New South Wales, Australia, on May 31, 1991.

Oldest groom: 103-year-old Harry Stevens, wed to 84-year-old Thelma Lucas, his cousin, at the Caravilla Retirement Home in Beloit, Wisconsin, on December 3, 1984.

Oldest matron of honor: Flossie Bennett, who was 97 years and 181 days old at the February 6, 1999, wedding of Edna and Leonard Petchey in Holton, England.

AN UNDERGROUND WEDDING

▼ ▼

With their cathedral-like caverns and stalactite and stalagmite formations resembling organ pipes or stately columns, many caves around the world have been viewed as possible wedding venues down through the centuries. One such place, the Gothic Chapel in Kentucky's Mammoth Cave, saw some 16 weddings held there between 1851 and 1915 (weddings have not been allowed there since it became a national park in 1941). Joseph Parrish, M.D., described the setting and its first official nuptials in his book *The Mammoth Cave of Kentucky: An Address Delivered Before the Young Men's Association of Burlington, New Jersey, January 1852*:

> Next, we enter a large elliptical-shaped room, called Gothic Chapel, with the richest stalactites festooning the ceiling, and falling in heavy columns to the floor of the apartment. In the center of the chapel, four columns unite at the top and seem to be designed to support the great arch.
>
> Under the principal arch stands the arm chair, a union of stalactite growth of this shape, in which a person may sit with tolerable ease; the pillars of the chair uniting at the top and forming an irregular canopy, reaching to the ceiling.
>
> The cave guide takes away the lights, ascends to a high gallery, and illuminates the whole apartment with a Bengal light. Its arched ceiling, fluted walls, and heavy pillars, blending together to perfect the style, are brought out in full view, and the beholder can scarcely realize that nature has been so bountiful in her displays of wonder, so far down, below the surface of the earth.
>
> But, so it is, the hand that clothed the landscape with beauty to gratify the eye and improve the taste has arched out of the bosom of the earth the richest architectural designs, to exalt the soul of man above himself and inspire his heart with gratitude. During the last month, this place has, for the first time within our knowledge, been appropriated for the accomplishment of the marriage ceremony. The following, from the Louisville Journal, is presented as evidence of the fact:
>
> "Married, on the 29th of April, in the Gothic Chapel of the Mammoth Cave of Kentucky, by the Rev. Dr. Edgar, of Nashville,

Tennessee: the Rev. J. H. Hall, of Bourbon County, to Miss Wealthy F. Pettingill, of Winthrop, Maine. The ceremony, we are told, was exceedingly solemn and impressive. After it was over, some beautiful verses by Mrs. Lydia H. Sigourney, written for the occasion, were sung by the party, consisting of some 50 or 60 ladies and gentlemen."

RANDOM STATS, PART XVII: PREMARITAL COHABITATION

▼▼

16 percent: Australian couples in 1965 that cohabited before marriage.

72 percent: Australian couples in 2001 that cohabited before marriage.

71 percent: Weddings in England and Wales in 1998 for which participants gave identical premarriage residential addresses.

73 percent: Weddings in England and Wales in 1999 for which participants gave identical premarriage residential addresses.

75 percent: Weddings in England and Wales in 2000 for which participants gave identical premarriage residential addresses.

84 percent: Civil-ceremony weddings in England and Wales in 1998 for which participants gave identical premarriage residential addresses.

85 percent: Civil-ceremony weddings in England and Wales in 1999 for which participants gave identical premarriage residential addresses.

86 percent: Civil-ceremony weddings in England and Wales in 2000 for which participants gave identical premarriage residential addresses.

51 percent: Religious-ceremony weddings in England and Wales in 1998 for which participants gave identical premarriage residential addresses.

53 percent: Religious-ceremony weddings in England and Wales in 1999 for which participants gave identical premarriage residential addresses.

56 percent: Religious-ceremony weddings in England and Wales in 2000 for which participants gave identical premarriage residential addresses.

ULTIMATE MARRIAGE

▼▼

The old ideals are dead as nails—nothing there. It seems to me there remains only this perfect union with a woman—sort of ultimate marriage—and there isn't anything else.

—*Women in Love* (1920), D. H. Lawrence

SOME CLASSIC CARTOON WEDDINGS

▼▼▼

Seek out these and other classics on video and DVD collections:

Rabbit of Seville (1950): In one of the greatest of all Looney Tunes from Warner Bros., directed by Chuck Jones, Elmer Fudd chases Bugs Bunny into the Hollywood Bowl, where they take over an open-air production of Rossini's *The Barber of Seville,* ending with a thoroughly befuddled Elmer as the bride and Bugs as the groom.

Hare Trimmed (1953): Yosemite Sam courts the wealthy widow Emma, and Bugs decides to court her too, just to stymie Sam. Of course, Sam almost winds up marrying Bugs by accident.

The Simpsons, **"Black Widower"** (airdate April 9, 1992): Just out of prison, Sideshow Bob (Kelsey Grammer) marries Selma (Julie Kavner) as part of his plan to do away with nemesis Bart Simpson (Nancy Cartwright).

> *"Inspired by the love of a good woman, I resolved*
> *to be the best darned Inmate #24601 I could be."*
> —Sideshow Bob

The Simpsons, **"Lisa's Wedding"** (airdate March 19, 1995): Lisa Simpson (Yeardley Smith) encounters a fortune-teller who casts her imagination forward to her romance with and engagement to a brilliant and handsome English aristocrat, Hugh Parkfield (Mandy Patinkin). The wedding goes awry, of course, at the hands of Homer (Dan Castellaneta).

> *"Homer, don't take this wrong, but I've obtained a court order*
> *preventing you from planning this wedding."*
> —Marge Simpson (Julie Kavner)

The Simpsons, **"The Two Mrs. Nahasapeemapetilons"** (airdate November 16, 1997): Quik-E-Mart owner Apu Nahasapeemapetilon (Hank Azaria) tries to avoid his impending arranged marriage to Manjula (Jan Hooks) by pretending that he is already married to Marge Simpson (Julie Kavner), before falling in love with his betrothed and having a gala Hindu ceremony in the Simpsons' backyard.

SOME HUMOROUS MARRIAGE QUOTES

▼▼▼

Let us now set forth one of the fundamental truths about marriage: the wife is in charge.　　　　　　　　—*Love and Marriage* (1989), Bill Cosby

❧

Marriage is the alliance of two people, one of whom never remembers birthdays and the other who never forgets them.
　　　　　　　　　　　　　　　　　　—Ogden Nash (1902–1971)

❧

A man in love is incomplete until he is married. Then he's finished.
　　　　　　　　　　　　　　　　　　—Zsa Zsa Gabor (born 1917)

❧

I love being married. It's so great to find that one special person you want to annoy for the rest of your life.　　　　　　—Rita Rudner (born 1956)

❧

They say love is blind and marriage is an institution. Well, I'm not ready for an institution for the blind just yet.　　—Mae West (1892/1893–1980)

❧

Don't marry for money. You can borrow it cheaper.　　—Scottish proverb

❧

An archaeologist is the best husband a woman can have; the older she gets the more interested he is in her.　　—Agatha Christie (1890–1976)

❧

I was the best man at the wedding. If I'm the best man, why is she marrying him?　　　　　　　　　　　　　　　　—Jerry Seinfeld (born 1954)

MAID OR MATRON OF HONOR'S RESPONSIBILITIES

♥ ♥

Being maid or matron of honor is not an honor alone; it's a responsibility, or rather many of them. Here are some of the most common duties, compiled from many sources and from personal experience.

- Help the bride as necessary through the planning and organization of the wedding.
- Help organize the fitting of bridesmaids' dresses.
- Host a shower or other pre-wedding party.
- Greet the officiant and direct him or her to the venue for the wedding ceremony.
- Help the bride stay calm and focused, or diverted, before the ceremony.
- Escorted by the best man, precede the bride down the aisle.
- Help the bride with her veil or train as the ceremony begins.
- Hold the bridal bouquet during the ceremony, returning it to the bride before she walks back up the aisle.
- Keep track of the groom's ring.
- Sign the marriage license or certificate as witness.
- Look after the bride, anticipating and fulfilling her needs, throughout the wedding party.
- Dance with the best man, followed by the groom, at the wedding party.
- Assist the best man, bridesmaids, and groomsmen in decorating the going-away vehicle, while keeping it safe to drive.
- Help the bride change into her going-away outfit.

TO CONFOUND AND DELIGHT

♥ ♥

May heaven grant you everything your heart desires: a husband, a house, and a happy, peaceful home. For there is nothing nobler or more admirable than when a man and a woman who see eye-to-eye keep house as man and wife. It confounds their enemies and delights their friends—but they themselves know more about it than anyone.

—*The Odyssey* (eighth century BC), Homer

BEST MAN'S RESPONSIBILITIES

▼▼▼

Being the groom's best man involves more than just planning the bachelor party and making a toast. Here are some classic duties, compiled from many sources and from personal experience.

- Host the bachelor's party.
- Ensure that all groomsmen are properly dressed and accessorized before wedding photography and the ceremony.
- Help the groom dress and stay neat before, during, and after the ceremony.
- Keep all groomsmen together and ready.
- Help the groom stay calm and focused, or diverted, before the ceremony.
- Keep track of the wedding license and any other documentation.
- Keep track of the bride's ring.
- Escort the maid or matron of honor.
- Stand beside the groom during the ceremony, assisting with the rings if necessary.
- Sign the marriage license or certificate as witness.
- Pay the officiant on behalf of the groom.
- Compose or select and deliver the first toast to the married couple.
- Collect congratulatory messages from those who were unable to attend, and read them aloud at the reception.
- Collect and safeguard any gifts of money for the couple.
- Assist the maid or matron of honor, bridesmaids, and groomsmen in decorating the going-away vehicle, while keeping it safe to drive.
- Ensure return of all men's rental clothing.

SING OUT!

▼▼▼

I sing of brooks, of blossoms, birds, and bowers:
Of April, May, of June, and July-flowers.
I sing of May-poles, hock-carts, wassails, wake,
Of bride-grooms, brides, and of their bridal-cakes.
— "The Argument of His Book," *Hesperides* (1648),
Robert Herrick

THE TAJ MAHAL

No other creation rivals the Taj Mahal as a gesture of romantic love. The fifth Mughal emperor, Shah Jahan, built it at Agra, India, in tribute to his second wife, Mumtaz Mahal. She died in 1631 after giving birth to their 14th child, but not before receiving her husband's promise of the palace. Work began that year and, with 20,000 builders and 1,000 elephants transporting materials, the white marble building took 22 years to complete. Mumtaz and Shah Jahan are buried side by side within.

HUMBLE NUPTIALS

What need of clamorous bells, or ribands gay,
These humble nuptials to proclaim or grace?
Angels of love, look down upon the place;
Shed on the chosen vale a sun-bright day!
—"Composed on the Eve of the Marriage of a Friend
in the Vale of Grasmere" (1812), William Wordsworth

A PROPOSAL ETCHED IN WOOD

The bridges of Madison County, Iowa, made famous in the book by Robert James Waller and the Clint Eastwood–Meryl Streep movie based on it, have offered shy young Midwestern men an alternative way to state their intentions since the early years of the 20th century. Some of those historic bridges bear evidence of proposals carved with penknives inside the wooden structures, including this inscription on the vintage 1883 Roseman Bridge: "In life we will cross many bridges, some covered, others not."

STRAIGHT TO THE HEART

In most cultures today, married people wear their wedding rings on the third finger of the left hand. The reason for this practice traces back to ancient Egypt, where wedding rings were first exchanged and worn on that particular digit in the belief that a vein went directly from it to the heart.

WEDDINGS BY THE MONTH

▼▼▼

Married when **the year is new**, he'll be loving, kind and true.
When **February** birds do mate, you wed nor dread your fate.
If you wed when **March** winds blow, joy and sorrow both you'll know.
Marry in **April** when you can, joy for Maiden and for Man.
Marry in the month of **May**, surely you will rue the day.
Marry when **June** roses grow, over land and sea you'll go.
Those who in **July** do wed, labor for their daily bred.
Whoever wed in **August** be, many a change is sure to see.
Marry in **September**'s shrine, live a life that's rich and fine.
If in **October** you do marry, love will come but riches tarry.
If you wed in bleak **November**, only joys will come, remember.
When **December** snows fall fast, marry and true love will last.

—Old English folk rhyme

THE SEVEN HUSBANDS (AND EIGHT MARRIAGES) OF ELIZABETH TAYLOR

▼▼▼

1. **Nicky Hilton Jr.**, hotel chain heir (married 1950–1951)
2. **Michael Wilding**, actor (1952–1956)
3. **Mike Todd**, movie producer (1957–1958)*
4. **Eddie Fisher**, singer (1959–1964)
5. **Richard Burton**, actor (1964–1974)
6. **Richard Burton**, actor (1975–1976)
7. **John Warner**, United States Senator (1976–1982)**
8. **Larry Fortensky**, construction worker (1991–1996)

* Todd was the only husband Taylor did not divorce. He died tragically on
March 23, 1958, in the New Mexico crash of his private airplane, the *Lucky Liz*.
** Between her marriages to John Warner and Larry Fortensky, Taylor was
engaged twice, first to attorney Victor Luna (engagement broken in 1984), then
to businessman Dennis Stein (broken in 1985).

A PERILOUS REMEDY AND A SETTLED HABIT
▼▼

Marriage is terrifying, but so is a cold and forlorn old age. The friendships of men are vastly agreeable, but they are insecure. You know all the time that one friend will marry and put you to the door; a second accept a situation in China, and become no more to you than a name, a reminiscence, and an occasional crossed letter, very laborious to read; a third will take up with some religious crotchet and treat you to sour looks thence-forward. So, in one way or another, life forces men apart and breaks up the goodly fellowships for ever. . . . Marriage is certainly a perilous remedy. Instead of on two or three, you stake your happiness on one life only. But still, as the bargain is more explicit and complete on your part, it is more so on the other; and you have not to fear so many contingencies; it is not every wind that can blow you from your anchorage; and so long as Death withholds his sickle, you will always have a friend at home. . . . The discretion of the first years becomes the settled habit of the last; and so, with wisdom and patience, two lives may grow indissolubly into one.

—*Virginibus Puerisque* (1876–1879), Robert Louis Stevenson

EXTREME WEDDINGS
▼▼

Looking for a different, thrilling, possibly even dangerous way to exchange vows? Consider some of the following actual wedding options.

Bungee jumping: With strong elastic cords attached to your feet at one end and a solid anchorage at the other, leap side-by-side off a high bridge as you say your "I dooooooooooooossssssssssss!!!!!"

Helicopter: Hover over city or countryside—just you, an officiant, the requisite witnesses, and of course the pilot.

Scuba diving: If you're both certified divers, you can literally take the plunge, making a dive—complete with vows conducted using hand signals—the central part of the wedding ceremony.

Skiing: Avid snow sports enthusiasts can ski to a scenic spot for the exchange of vows, immediately followed by a tandem run down the slopes.

Skydiving: The minister or justice of the peace jumps along with you so you can exchange vows in midair.

Waterskiing: Vows are exchanged at the shore or dockside, immediately after which bride and groom are whisked away across the water at the end of his-and-her towlines.

THE EIGHT MARRIAGES OF MICKEY ROONEY

▼▼

"My partners weren't what we call in horse-racing parlance routers," says actor Mickey Rooney (born 1920). "They were sprinters; they went out of the gate, but then they stopped. They couldn't go the distance."

1. **Ava Gardner**, actress (married 1942–1943)
2. **Betty Jane Rase**, beauty queen (1944–1948)
3. **Martha Vickers**, actress (1948–1951)
4. **Elaine Mahnken**, model (1952–1958)
5. **Barbara Ann Thomason**, beauty queen and actress (1958–1966)*
6. **Marge Lane**, (1967)**
7. **Carolyn Hockett**, (1969–1974)
8. **January "Jan" Chamberlin**, singer (1978–present)

* Killed by her lover Milos Milocevic in a murder-suicide.
** Best friend of Barbara Ann Thomason. Marriage lasted 100 days.

FALLING IN LOVE, AGAIN

▼▼

A successful marriage requires falling in love many times, always with the same person.   —Germaine Greer (born 1939)

RANDOM STATS, PART XVIII

▼▼

$19 billion: Annual U.S. retail revenues through bridal registries.
$4 billion: Amount spent annually on household furniture by engaged couples in the United States.
$3 billion: Amount spent annually on housewares by engaged couples in the United States.
$400 million: Amount spent annually on tableware by engaged couples in the United States.

SOME INNOVATIVE WEDDING CAKE FLAVORS

♥♥

Many couples today consider having different flavors for different tiers of cake (see "Wedding Cake Sizes and Servings," page 42), and add even more variety with similarly innovative fillings and icings. Here are some flavors you may want to consider.

- Amaretto
- Apple pecan
- Banana walnut
- Bellini
  (peach and champagne)
- Butter mint
- Butter pecan
- Buttermilk spice
- Cappuccino
- Cherry almond
- Chocolate cherry
- Chocolate mint
- Chocolate orange
- Chocolate peanut butter
- Chocolate raspberry
- Chocolate walnut
- Devil's food
- German chocolate
- Grand Marnier
- Hazelnut praline
- Kahlua
- Key lime
- Lemon poppy seed
- Macadamia nut
- Orange almond
- Peaches and cream
- Piña colada
- Pistachio
- Raspberry and cream
- Tangerine orange zest
- White chocolate cherry

SOME POLISH WEDDING CUSTOMS

♥♥

Passing of the veil: After the wedding, on her own or with her mother's help, the bride will remove her veil, passing it along to the maid of honor or other bridesmaids to bring them good luck in finding a mate.

Capping: Sometimes the mother of the bride or another older woman will then place upon the bride's head a *czypek*, a traditional lace woman's bonnet, signifying her new role.

Bread, salt, wine, and silver: The parents of the bride and groom give them bread, which the couple eats to ensure that they won't go hungry; salt, which they taste together so they will help each other overcome life's bitterness; wine, which they sip together as they will enjoy life's sweetness; and a silver coin, which they grasp for good fortune.

Buying a bridal dance: During the wedding celebration, guests may buy a dance with the bride, pinning money to her veil or dress or presenting it to one of the bridesmaids for safekeeping in a special purse, basket, or bowl.

HONEY-MOONING FOR A YEAR

♥♥♥

Had he ever thought it all out? she asked. No. Well, she had; and would he kindly not interrupt? In the first place, there would be all the wedding-presents. Jewels, and a motor, and a silver dinner service, did she mean? Not a bit of it! She could see he'd never given the question proper thought. Cheques, my dear, nothing but cheques—she undertook to manage that on her side: she really thought she could count on about fifty, and she supposed he could rake up a few more? Well, all that would simply represent pocket-money! For they would have plenty of houses to live in: he'd see. People were always glad to lend their house to a newly-married couple. It was such fun to pop down and see them: it made one feel romantic and jolly. All they need do was to accept the houses in turn: go on honey-mooning for a year! What was he afraid of? Didn't he think they'd be happy enough to want to keep it up? And why not at least try— get engaged, and then see what would happen? Even if she was all wrong, and her plan failed, wouldn't it have been rather nice, just for a month or two, to fancy they were going to be happy?

—*The Glimpses of the Moon* (1922), Edith Wharton

RANDOM STATS, PART XIX: U.S. WEDDING MONTH POPULARITY

♥♥♥

10.8 percent: Weddings held in June.
10.2 percent: Weddings held in August.
9.8 percent: Weddings held in May.
9.7 percent: Weddings held in July.
9.6 percent: Weddings held in September.
9.4 percent: Weddings held in October.
7.8 percent: Weddings held in December.
7.4 percent: Weddings held in April.
7.4 percent: Weddings held in November (tied with April).
7 percent: Weddings held in February.
6.1 percent: Weddings held in March.
4.7 percent: Weddings held in January.

SOME FAMOUS LAS VEGAS WEDDINGS

♥♥♥

The combination of no state waiting period for marriage licenses, legalized gambling since 1931, resort-style casino hotels, and proximity to Hollywood has long made Las Vegas a celebrity wedding destination. Here is a selection of many held there.

1931

Silent film star **Clara Bow** and cowboy film star **Rex Bell**

1933

Actress **Lupe Velez** and actor/Olympic star **Johnny Weissmuller**

1943

Actress **Betty Grable** and bandleader/trumpet-player **Harry James**
(at Little Church of the West)

1946

Actress **Evelyn Keyes** and director **John Huston**

1953

Actress **Rita Hayworth** and singer **Dick Haymes** (at Sands Hotel)

1954

Publicist **Ann Buydens** and actor **Kirk Douglas** (at Sahara Hotel)

1955

Actress **Joan Crawford** and pepsi Chairman **Alfred Steele**
(at Flamingo Hotel)

1958

Actress **Joanne Woodward** and actor **Paul Newman**
(at El Rancho Hotel)

1965

Actress **Dyan Cannon** and actor **Cary Grant** (at Dunes Hotel)

Singer/actress **Judy Garland** and actor **Mark Harron**
(at Little Church of the West)

1966
Singer/actor **Frank Sinatra** and actress **Mia Farrow** (at Sands Hotel)

1967
Singer **Elvis Presley** and **Patricia Anne Beaulieu** (at Aladdin Hotel)

1971
Singer **Diana Ross** and businessman **Robert Silverstein**
(at Silver Bells Chapel)

1973
Actor **Michael Caine** and model **Shakira Baksh**

1985
Singer/actress **Bette Midler** and commodities broker/performer
Martin von Hasselberg (at Candlelight Wedding Chapel)

Actress **Joan Collins** and singer **Peter Holm** (at Little White Chapel)

1988
Actor **Dudley Moore** and actress **Brogan Lane**
(at Little Church of the West)

1991
Actor **Richard Gere** and model **Cindy Crawford**

1996
Actor/director **Clint Eastwood** and newswoman **Dina Ruiz**

1998
Actor **Tony Curtis** and horse trainer **Jill Vanden Berg**
(at MGM Grand Hotel)

2000
Dixie Chicks singer **Natalie Maines** and actor **Adrian Pasdar**
(at Little White Chapel)

2004
Singer **Britney Spears** and college junior **Jason Alexander**
(at Little White Chapel)

LANGUAGE OF FLOWERS

▼▼

Down through history, emotional and spiritual meanings have been ascribed to flowers, with the best-known chronicler of these being the Englishwoman Kate Greenaway in her *Language of Flowers* (1885). Such meanings, summarized below from a variety of sources, may be used to convey a personal message at a wedding, whether in the bouquets held by the bride or her bridesmaids, the petals strewn by the flower girls, the groom's or groomsmen's boutonnieres, or the arrangements in the ceremony or banquet venues. Those who are superstitious may take note, and beware, of those flowers deemed to convey negative meanings.

Flower	Meaning
Allyssum	Worth beyond beauty
Ambrosia	Love returned
Anemone	Anticipation, expectation
Aster	Love, daintiness
Baby's breath	Enduring love
Bachelor's buttons	Celibacy, hope
Bluebells	Constancy, kindness
Buttercups	Cheer, childishness, ingratitude
Calendulas	Joy
Camellias	Admiration, gratitude, pity
Carnations, pink	Remembrance
Carnations, purple	Capriciousness, whimsy
Carnations, red	Admiration, heartache
Carnations, striped	Refusal
Carnations, white	Innocence
Carnations, yellow	Disdain, rejection
Cherry blossoms	Spiritual beauty
Chrysanthemums, red	Love
Chrysanthemums, white	Truth
Chrysanthemums, yellow	Slighted love
Columbine, purple	Resolve
Columbine, red	Anxiety
Cowslips	Pensiveness
Crocuses	Cheer
Cyclamen	Resignation

Flower	Meaning
Daffodils	Chivalry, respect
Daisies	Innocence
Dandelions	Coquetry
Delphiniums	Lightness, swiftness
Forget-me-nots	True love
Fuchsia	Taste
Gardenias	Ecstasy, grace, secret love
Gerbera daisies	Beauty
Geraniums	Silliness
Gladiolas	Love at first sight
Heather, lavender	Admiration, solitude
Heather, white	Protection, dream-come-true
Heliotropes	Adoration, devotion
Hibiscus	Delicate beauty
Honeysuckles	Devoted affection
Hyacinths, blue	Constancy
Hyacinths, purple	Sorrow
Hyacinths, pink	Playfulness
Hyacinths, white	Loveliness
Hyacinths, yellow	Jealousy
Hydrangeas	Boastfulness, heartlessness
Irises	Faith, hope, wisdom
Jasmine, white	Amiability, wealth
Jasmine, yellow	Elegance, grace
Jonquils	Desire, sympathy
Lavender	Devotion, distrust, mistrust
Lilacs	Love
Lilies, calla	Beauty, delicacy, modesty
Lilies, day	Coquetry
Lilies, orange	Hatred
Lilies, tiger	Pride, wealth
Lilies, white	Purity, virginity
Lilies, yellow	Gaiety, falseness
Lilies of the valley	Humility, sweetness
Marigolds	Chagrin, grief, solace
Narcissus	Egotism
Nasturtiums	Charity, patriotism, victory

Flower	Meaning
Orange blossoms	Chastity, wisdom
Orchids	Beauty, love, refinement
Pansies	Loving thoughts
Peach blossoms	Devotion, longevity
Peonies	Passion
Periwinkles	Sweet memories
Petunias	Anger, resentment
Poppies, red	Consolation, pleasure
Poppies, white	Consolation, sleep
Poppies, yellow	Success, wealth
Primroses	Yearning
Primroses, evening	Inconstancy
Rosemary	Remembrance, fidelity
Rosebuds	Innocent love
Rosebuds, red	Pure love
Rosebuds, white	Girlhood
Roses, pink	Perfect happiness
Roses, red	Desire, love
Roses, red and white	Togetherness
Roses, tea	Remembrance
Roses, thornless	Love at first sight
Roses, white	Eternal love, innocence
Roses, yellow	Jealousy
Salvia	Thinking of you
Snapdragons	Deception, presumption
Snowdrops	Consolation, hope
Stephanotis	Happy marriage, travel
Sunflowers	Loyalty, good wishes
Sweet peas	Bliss, departure
Thyme	Courage, strength
Tulips, red	Belief, I love you
Tulips, yellow	Unrequited love
Violets	Calmness, modesty
Violets, blue	Faithful, watchful
Zinnias, magenta	Lasting affection
Zinnias, scarlet	Constancy
Zinnias, white	Goodness
Zinnias, yellow	Remembrance

DIAMOND SUBSTITUTES

♥♥♥

Although nothing compares to the dazzle and quality of a real diamond, look-alikes for the classic wedding gem find favor among those who cannot afford the real thing.

The mineral known as zircon, scientifically known as zirconium silicate or $ZrSiO_4$, is a crystal found in a range of colors, which can be heat-treated to become colorless. Hard, though not as hard as a diamond, and with good sparkle, it has long stood in for diamonds in inexpensive rings.

Not to be confused with the zircon, which is found in nature, is the laboratory-produced cubic zirconia, now generally marketed as "CZ" or a "CZ diamond." Produced through a process that was developed in the 1970s by a Russian scientist, the gem is made by heating together zirconium oxide and yttrium oxide to a temperature approaching 5,000°F (2,760°C). Swarovski and Co. began marketing these gems during the 1980s, and they have found favor not only for their price but also for their outstanding beauty, clarity, and hardness, though none of their qualities approach those of true diamonds.

SHEAR COMPANIONSHIP

♥♥♥

Marriage resembles a pair of shears, so joined that they cannot be separated; often moving in opposite directions, yet always punishing anyone who comes between them. —Sydney Smith (1771–1845)

RANDOM STATS, PART XX

♥♥♥

14 months: Length of average engagement in the United States.
Over 20 and rising: Percent of gowns purchased in the United States from David's Bridal, the largest national chain.
35: Percent of brides and grooms holding valid U.S. passports.
55 to 70 percent: Rate of intermarriage among blood relatives in some tribal areas of southern Saudi Arabia.
55 percent: Australian weddings now held as civil ceremonies.
40 percent: Australian weddings held as civil ceremonies circa 1984.

SOME BRIEF CELEBRITY MARRIAGES

▼▼▼

Modern-day marriage milestones, in descending order of duration:

2 years: Singer **Paula Abdul** and actor **Emilio Estevez** (1992–1994).

21 months: Actress **Julia Roberts** and country star **Lyle Lovett** (1993–1995).

20 months: Singer/Elvis heir **Lisa Marie Presley** and "King of Pop" **Michael Jackson** (1994–1996).

17 months: Singer **Paula Abdul** and clothing manufacturer **Brad Beckerman** (1996–1998).

16 months: Singer/actress **Liza Minnelli** and producer **David Gest** (2002–2003).

13 months: Actress/singer **Jennifer Lopez** and model/actor **Ojani Noa** (1997–1998).

11 months: Actress **Helen Hunt** and actor **Hank Azaria** (1999–2000).

10 months: Actress **Alyssa Milano** and musician **Cinjun Tate** (1999).

10 months: Actress **Lauren Holly** and actor **Jim Carrey** (1996–1997).

9 months: Actress/singer **Jennifer Lopez** and dancer/choreographer **Cris Judd** (2002)

9 months: Actress **Shannen Doherty** and Internet entrepreneur **Rick Salomon** (2002).

8 months: Actress **Elizabeth Taylor** [see "The Seven Husbands (and Eight Marriages) of Elizabeth Taylor," page 149] and hotel heir **Nicky Hilton** (1950–1951).

7 months: Actress **Courtney Thorne-Smith** and scientist **Andrew Conrad** (2000–2001).

7 months: Model **Erin Everly** and rock star **Axl Rose** (1990).

7 months: Model **Christie Brinkley** and real estate developer **Ricky Taubman** (1994–1995).

5 months: Actress **Drew Barrymore** and comedian **Tom Green** (2001).

5 months: Actress **Carmen Electra** and basketball star **Dennis Rodman** (1998).

4 months: Actress **Shannen Doherty** and actor **Ashley Hamilton** (1993–1994).

4 months: Singer **Janet Jackson** and singer **James DeBarge** (1984).

3½ months: Singer/Elvis heir **Lisa Marie Presley** and actor **Nicolas Cage** (2002–2003).

32 days: Singer/actress **Ethel Merman** and actor **Ernest Borgnine** (1964).

30 days: Actress **Drew Barrymore** and bar owner **Jeremy Thomas** (1994).

12 days: Actress **Catherine Oxenberg** and producer **Robert Evans** (1998).

9 days: Singer/actress **Cher** and rocker **Gregg Allman** (1977).

8 days: Singer **Michelle Phillips** and actor **Dennis Hopper** (1971).

55 hours: Singer **Britney Spears** and college junior **Jason Alexander** (2004).

1 day: Actress **Zsa Zsa Gabor** (see "The Nine Husbands of Zsa Zsa Gabor," page 37) and lawyer **Felipe de Alba** (1982).

Less than 1 day: Actress **Robin Givens** and tennis player **Svetozar Marinkovic** (August 22, 1997).

6 hours: Actor **Rudolph Valentino** and actress **Jean Acker** (November 5, 1919).

YOUNG LOVE ON THE MISSISSIPPI

▼▼

He turned his face away. She bent timidly around till her breath stirred his curls and whispered, "I—love—you!"

Then she sprang away and ran around and around the desks and benches, with Tom after her, and took refuge in a corner at last, with her little white apron to her face. Tom clasped her about her neck and pleaded:

"Now, Becky, it's all done—all over but the kiss. Don't you be afraid of that—it ain't anything at all. Please, Becky." And he tugged at her apron and the hands.

By and by she gave up, and let her hands drop; her face, all glowing with the struggle, came up and submitted. Tom kissed the red lips and said:

"Now it's all done, Becky. And always after this, you know, you ain't ever to love anybody but me, and you ain't ever to marry anybody but me, ever never and forever. Will you?"

"No, I'll never love anybody but you, Tom, and I'll never marry anybody but you—and you ain't to ever marry anybody but me, either."

"Certainly. Of course. That's PART of it. And always coming to school or when we're going home, you're to walk with me, when there ain't anybody looking—and you choose me and I choose you at parties, because that's the way you do when you're engaged."

—*The Adventures of Tom Sawyer* (1881), Mark Twain

SOME WEDDING AND MARITAL BUMPER STICKERS

❤❤❤

Driver carries no cash—he's married.

Forget your anniversary once.
Remember it forever.

Husband: Someone who takes out the trash while
giving the impression he cleaned the whole house.

I am not a bum. My wife works!

I don't need kids. I married one.

*

I got this motor home/trailer/car/truck for my wife.
Best deal I ever made!

I married my wife for her looks,
but not the ones she's been giving me lately.

If marriage were outlawed,
only outlaws would have in-laws.

[On a motorcycle:] If you can read this, my wife fell off.

I'm the man of the house—
and I have my wife's permission to say so!

It used to be wine, women, and song.
Now it's beer, the old lady, and TV.

Love is blind.
Marriage is a real eye-opener.

Marine wife.
Toughest job in the Corps.

Marriage: A word, not a sentence.

❦

Marriage is an institution.
I'm not ready to be institutionalized.

❦

Married by a judge.
Should have asked for a jury.*

❦

Married people live longer than single people.
Or maybe it just seems longer.

❦

Men with pierced ears are ready for marriage:
They've experienced pain and bought jewelry.

❦

My husband says if I read one more romance novel,
he's going to leave me. Gosh, I'll miss him.

❦

My wife complains that I never listen to her
. . . or something like that.

❦

My wife says if I go fishing one more time,
she's going to leave me. Gosh, I'll miss her.

❦

Someday my prince will come.
He just took a wrong turn and is too stubborn to ask for directions.

❦

We're staying together for the sake of the cats.

❦

When I married Mr. Right,
I had no idea his first name was Always.

❦

Why don't men ask for advice on
how to combine marriage and a career?

*A variation on a quote from comedian Groucho Marx (1890–1977):
"I was married by a judge. I should have asked for a jury."

A FLUSTERED, HAPPY, HURRIED DREAM

♥♥

Yes! I am going to be married to Dora! Miss Lavinia and Miss Clarissa have given their consent; and if ever canary birds were in a flutter, they are. Miss Lavinia, self-charged with the superintendence of my darling's wardrobe, is constantly cutting out brown-paper cuirasses, and differing in opinion from a highly respectable young man, with a long bundle, and a yard measure under his arm. A dressmaker, always stabbed in the breast with a needle and thread, boards and lodges in the house; and seems to me, eating, drinking, or sleeping, never to take her thimble off. They make a lay-figure of my dear. They are always sending for her to come and try something on. We can't be happy together for five minutes in the evening, but some intrusive female knocks at the door, and says, 'Oh, if you please, Miss Dora, would you step upstairs!'

Miss Clarissa and my aunt roam all over London, to find out articles of furniture for Dora and me to look at. It would be better for them to buy the goods at once, without this ceremony of inspection; for, when we go to see a kitchen fender and meat-screen, Dora sees a Chinese house for Jip, with little bells on the top, and prefers that. And it takes a long time to accustom Jip to his new residence, after we have bought it; whenever he goes in or out, he makes all the little bells ring, and is horribly frightened.

Peggotty comes up to make herself useful, and falls to work immediately. Her department appears to be, to clean everything over and over again. She rubs everything that can be rubbed, until it shines, like her own honest forehead, with perpetual friction. And now it is, that I begin to see her solitary brother passing through the dark streets at night, and looking, as he goes, among the wandering faces. I never speak to him at such an hour. I know too well, as his grave figure passes onward, what he seeks, and what he dreads.

Why does Traddles look so important when he calls upon me this afternoon in the Commons—where I still occasionally attend, for form's sake, when I have time? The realization of my boyish day-dreams is at hand. I am going to take out the licence.

It is a little document to do so much; and Traddles contemplates it, as it lies upon my desk, half in admiration, half in awe. There are the names, in the sweet old visionary connexion, David Copperfield and Dora Spenlow; and there, in the corner, is that Parental Institution, the Stamp

Office, which is so benignantly interested in the various transactions of human life, looking down upon our Union; and there is the Archbishop of Canterbury invoking a blessing on us in print, and doing it as cheap as could possibly be expected.

Nevertheless, I am in a dream, a flustered, happy, hurried dream. I can't believe that it is going to be; and yet I can't believe but that everyone I pass in the street, must have some kind of perception, that I am to be married the day after tomorrow.

—*David Copperfield* (1850), Charles Dickens

PET WEDDINGS

♥♥

Although not sanctioned by law or by mainstream religious faiths, weddings for pets are becoming a hot fad among devoted owners (or, as some animal rights activists would have it, "human companions"). Consider some evidence:

- In September 1996, Wichan Jaratarcha held a wedding in Thailand's largest disco for his cats Phet and Ploy, who wore matching pink outfits for an occasion that cost the equivalent of $16,241.
- Two yellow Labradors—Hanna (in a white satin and tulle dress) and Alex (in a satin tux)—were wed in 2001 before 50 human and 12 canine guests, exchanging crystal collars in a ceremony held at the posh Beverly Hills Hotel.
- The Web site BeachWed.com offers the option of holding a wedding for pets on the beautiful surfside sands of Oahu, Hawaii, which will "bring more love into our lives and spread it to the universe."
- The Web site MarryYourPet.com, which bills itself as "the pet and people wedding specialists," offers a playful way for humans to hold commitment ceremonies with beloved animal companions, and includes a photo gallery of happy "couples."

FRIEND LIKE ME

♥♥♥

"Woman—Friend—Yes—I want Friend, like me."
—Frankenstein's Monster, *The Bride of Frankenstein* (1935),
screenplay by William Hurlbut

WEIRD LAWS: MARRIED LIFE

▼♥

A random compendium of archaic or just plain strange wedding-related laws still on the books. (See also "Weird Laws: Single Life," page 16; "Weird Laws: Courtship," page 82; and "Weird Laws: Weddings," page 125.)

No kissing! The city of **Hartford, Connecticut,** bars men from kissing their wives on Sunday.

No scowling! The city of **Detroit, Michigan,** bars men from scowling at their wives on Sunday.

No fishing! Married women may not fish alone on Sundays in the state of **Montana**.

Your ring is safe! Throughout most of the **United States**, wedding rings are protected from seizure by creditors in bankruptcies.

Your hair is mine! A woman's hair is her husband's legal property in the state of **Michigan**.

No booze without permission! In the state of **Pennsylvania**, women must give consent to their husbands' purchases of alcoholic beverages.

Hat, please! To buy a hat in the city of **Owensboro, Kentucky**, a woman must first receive her husband's permission.

Teeth, please! To wear false teeth in the state of **Vermont**, women must receive written permission from their husbands.

Stay out of his mail! The law forbids a woman from opening her husband's mail in the state of **Montana**.

Stay out of his pockets! The state of **Maryland** forbids a woman from going through her sleeping husband's pockets.

Look out! Cars driven by women must be preceded by their husbands waving red flags in **New Orleans, Louisiana,** and along Main Street in **Waynesboro, Virginia**.

No Coffee?! Failure to provide a wife with coffee in **Saudi Arabia** constitutes grounds for divorce.

AN UNFASHIONABLE, FAMILIAR WEDDING

♥▼♥

Meg looked very like a rose herself, for all that was best and sweetest in heart and soul seemed to bloom into her face that day, making it fair and tender, with a charm more beautiful than beauty. Neither silk, lace, nor orange flowers would she have. "I don't want a fashionable wedding, but only those about me whom I love, and to them I wish to look and be my familiar self."

So she made her wedding gown herself, sewing into it the tender hopes and innocent romances of a girlish heart. Her sisters braided up her pretty hair, and the only ornaments she wore were the lilies of the valley, which "her John" liked best of all the flowers that grew.

"You *do* look just like our own dear Meg, only so very sweet and lovely that I should hug you if it wouldn't crumple your dress," cried Amy, surveying her with delight when all was done.

"Then I am satisfied. But please hug and kiss me, everyone, and don't mind my dress. I want a great many crumples of this sort put into it today." And Meg opened her arms to her sisters, who clung about her with April faces for a minute, feeling that the new love had not changed the old.

—*Good Wives* (1869), Louisa May Alcott

RANDOM STATS, PART XXI

♥♥

5: Average number of bridesmaids at an American wedding.

5: Average number of groomsmen at an American wedding.

$50 billion: Annual spending on Japanese weddings.

23.9 percent: Food that goes to waste at average catered Japanese wedding banquet.

$70 billion: Spent annually in United States by couples to establish basics of married life such as insurance, cars, banking, and so on.

1 month: Average time of a Viking wedding feast.

99 percent: Couples who follow their weddings with honeymoons.

$12 billion: Annual retail dollar volume of the U.S. honeymoon industry.

1 week: Duration of average honeymoon.

254,400: Total number of weddings annually in Great Britain.

66 percent: British weddings held as civil ceremonies.

GOOD ADVICE

♥♥

My advice to you is to get married. If you find a good wife you'll be happy; if not, you'll become a philosopher. —Socrates (469–399 BC)

ANNIVERSARY GIFTS

♥♥

A wealth of tradition surrounds anniversary presents, and modern merchandising has given rise to even more gift-buying options. Bear in mind that creative interpretation can come into play for any gift: An ivory anniversary tribute could, for example, be a CD of piano music (as in "tickling the ivories"), or a paper anniversary gift could as easily be a framed poster or print as personalized stationery. Simple arithmetic can also yield solutions for years that don't have suggested traditional gifts, such as a 17th anniversary based on eighth plus ninth (pottery in a willow pattern?).

Anniversary	Traditional	Modern
First	Paper	Clocks
Second	Cotton	China
Third	Leather	Crystal/glass
Fourth	Linen/silk/fruit/flowers	Appliances
Fifth	Wood	Silverware
Sixth	Candy or iron	Wood
Seventh	Wool/copper	Desk sets
Eighth	Bronze or pottery	Linens/lace
Ninth	Pottery/china/willow	Leather
Tenth	Tin/aluminum	Diamond
Eleventh	Steel	Jewelry
Twelfth	Silk/linen	Pearls
Thirteenth	Lace	Textiles/furs
Fourteenth	Ivory	Gold jewelry
Fifteenth	Crystal	Watches
Sixteenth		Silver hollowware
Seventeenth		Furniture
Eighteenth		Porcelain
Nineteenth		Bronze
Twentieth	China	Platinum
Twenty-first		Brass/nickel
Twenty-second		Copper
Twenty-third		Silver plate
Twenty-fourth		Musical instruments
Twenty-fifth	Silver	Silver
Twenty-sixth		Original pictures

Anniversary	Traditional	Modern
Twenty-seventh		Sculpture
Twenty-eighth		Orchids
Twenty-ninth		New furniture
Thirtieth	Pearl	Diamond
Thirty-first		Timepieces
Thirty-second		Transportation
Thirty-third		Amethyst
Thirty-fourth		Opal
Thirty-fifth	Coral/jade	Jade
Thirty-sixth		Bone china
Thirty-seventh		Alabaster
Thirty-eighth		Beryl/tourmaline
Thirty-ninth		Lace
Fortieth	Ruby	Ruby
Forty-first		Land
Forty-second		Real estate
Forty-third		Travel
Forty-fourth		Groceries
Forty-fifth	Sapphire	Sapphire
Forty-sixth		Original poetry
Forty-seventh		Books
Forty-eighth		Opticals
Forty-ninth		Luxuries
Fiftieth	Gold	Gold
Fifty-fifth	Emerald	Emerald
Sixtieth	Diamond	Diamond
Seventy-fifth	Diamond/gold	Diamond/gold
Eightieth	Diamond/pearl	Diamond/pearl
Eighty-fifth	Diamond/sapphire	Diamond/sapphire
Ninetieth		Diamond/emerald
Ninety-fifth		Diamond/ruby
One hundredth		10-carat diamond

POINTS OF VIEW

♥♥♥

Love does not consist of gazing at each other, but in looking together in the same direction.   —Antoine de Saint-Exupery (1900–1944)

ONWARD THE BRIDAL PROCESSION

▼▼

This was the wedding morn of Priscilla the Puritan maiden.
Friends were assembled together; the Elder and Magistrate also
Graced the scene with their presence, and stood
like the Law and the Gospel,
One with the sanction of earth and one with the blessing of heaven.
Simple and brief was the wedding, as that of Ruth and of Boaz.
Softly the youth and the maiden repeated the words of betrothal,
Taking each other for husband and wife in the Magistrate's presence,
After the Puritan way, and the laudable custom of Holland.
Fervently then, and devoutly, the excellent Elder of Plymouth
Prayed for the hearth and the home, that were
founded that day in affection,
Speaking of life and of death, and imploring
Divine benedictions.

***

Onward the bridal procession now moved to their new habitation,
Happy husband and wife, and friends conversing together.
Pleasantly murmured the brook, as they crossed
the ford in the forest,
Pleased with the image that passed, like a dream of love,
through its bosom,
Tremulous, floating in air, o'er the depths of the azure abysses.
Down through the golden leaves the sun was pouring his splendors,
Gleaming on purple grapes, that, from branches
above them suspended,
Mingled their odorous breath with the balm
of the pine and the fir-tree,
Wild and sweet as the clusters that grew in the valley of Esheol.
Like a picture it seemed of the primitive, pastoral ages,
Fresh with the youth of the world, and recalling Rebecca and Isaac,
Old and yet ever new, and simple and beautiful always,
Love immortal and young in the endless succession of lovers.
So through the Plymouth woods passed onward
the bridal procession.

—"The Courtship of Miles Standish" (1858), Henry Wadsworth Longfellow

SOME WELSH WEDDING CUSTOMS

vvvvvvvvvvvvvvvvvvvvvvvvvvvvvvvvvvvvvvvvvvvvv

The bidding: A century or more ago, a *gwahaddwr*, or "bidder," would deliver to those on the guest list a personal wedding invitation, entering the home of each person carrying a brightly decorated willow staff that he knocked on the floor to gain attention before announcing the names of the betrothed and the wedding date. Each invited guest made a small contribution towards a cash fund that would be given to the newlyweds.

Pwrs a gwregys: "The purse and girdle" were household goods ranging from linens to cookware bestowed before the wedding upon the bride, along with money collected by the bidder.

Disguising the bride: In some parts of Wales, the groom and his grooms-men will find the home of the bride locked up tight when they arrive to collect her before the wedding ceremony. Their knocks and calls are greeted with the news that she isn't inside. When they are finally allowed to enter the house, the bride appears nowhere to be found among the many people inside. Finally, the search reveals her to be dressed in disguise as an old woman or a nursemaid.

Capturing the bride: As if that deception were not enough, when the bride finally arrives at the church with the groom, her father or broth-ers may seize her and carry her away by horseback or car. The groom chases after them, finally catches up, captures the bride, and brings her back to the church, where the ceremony at long last begins.

RANDOM STATS, PART XXII

vvvvvvvvvvvvvvvvvvvvvvvvvvvvvvvvvvvvvvvvvvvvv

42 percent: Brides who would keep their wedding the same size if they did it again.

37 percent: Brides who would have a smaller wedding.

21 percent: Brides who would have a bigger wedding.

A GOOD MARRIAGE

vvvvvvvvvvvvvvvvvvvvvvvvvvvvvvvvvvvvvvvvvvvvv

There is no more lovely, friendly, and charming a relationship, com-munion, or company than a good marriage.

—*Table Talk*, Martin Luther (1483–1546)

SPECIAL ANNIVERSARY MESSAGES

❤ ❤

Mark that special event with a special greeting from a head of state.

From the White House

American citizens who have just gotten married, or who are celebrating their 50th anniversary or a later one, can receive an official congratulatory greeting from the president of the United States. Send a letter of request to arrive at least six weeks before the event to The White House, Attn: Greetings Office, Washington, DC 20502-0039; fax it to the office at (202) 395-1232; or e-mail it to "White House Web Mail," easily located by typing that string of words into an Internet search engine. The White House will strive to send the greeting to arrive approximately 10 days before the event.

From Buckingham Palace

Citizens of Great Britain's "Realms or UK Overseas Territories" can receive a free congratulatory message for their 60th, 65th, and 70th wedding anniversary, and every year thereafter. All they need to do is complete a form available via the Web at www.royal.gov.uk and return it to the Anniversaries Office, Buckingham Palace, London SW1A 1AA, no sooner than three weeks before the anniversary. (Belated messages are also available up to six months after the date.)

Include with the form a legible photocopy of the marriage certificate and, for those living abroad or who were married overseas, proof of British nationality (a photocopy of the relevant pages of a current British passport).

From Canada's Office of the Prime Minister

Canadian citizens can receive a congratulatory letter marking their 25th, 30th, 35th, 40th, and 45th wedding anniversaries, or a congratulatory certificate for 50th anniversaries and up, by going online to www.pm.gc.ca and following instructions to fill out and submit an electronic Wedding Anniversary Congratulatory Message form; printing out and faxing in the form to (613) 941-6901; or writing a letter to the Coordinator, Congratulatory Message; Room 105—Langevin Block, Ottawa, Ontario K1A 0A2. Submit at least six weeks ahead of the anniversary.

From Australia's Office of the Prime Minister

Both the prime minister and the governor-general of Australia will send a special message to Australian couples "celebrating their 50th and subsequent wedding anniversaries." According to the official Australian government Web site, www.itsanhonour.gov.au, messages can be requested "up to two months before the big day" or up to a month after. Most thoughtfully, the government Web site suggests that, "To avoid distressing relatives when a recipient passes away in the meantime, it is advisable not to arrange messages more than two months in advance." Greetings can be delivered either to the recipients' home address or to another address.

Supporting documentation, such as marriage certificates and passports certifying citizenship, or a statutory declaration, must be submitted with requests. Applications should be submitted to local electorate offices or to the offices of the local federal member of parliament or senator. Appropriate requests to the prime minister will automatically be forwarded both to the governor-general's office and to Buckingham Palace.

From New Zealand's Government House

New Zealand's governor-general, prime minister, minister of internal affairs, minister for senior citizens, and local member of parliament, along with Buckingham Palace when appropriate (see above), will all send congratulatory messages for anniversaries in five-year increments starting with the 50th (60th for the reigning monarch) provided a Congratulatory Message Service Application Form has been completed and submitted at least one month before the occasion. The form is available from the Visits and Ceremonial Office, Department of Internal Affairs, PO Box 805, Wellington, New Zealand; or from Level 1, Bowen House, 1 Bowen Street, Wellington, New Zealand; or via the government Web site at www.dia.govt.nz. The form, along with a copy of the marriage certificate, can be mailed back to these addresses or faxed to 04 470 2909, marked "Attention: Congratulatory Message Service."

FRIENDSHIP EQUALS HAPPINESS

♥♥

It is not a lack of love but a lack of friendship that makes unhappy marriages.
—Friedrich Nietzsche (1844–1900)

SOME WEDDING AND MARRIAGE WEB SITES—IN THEIR OWN WORDS

♥♥♥

This list focuses on select Web sites that provide helpful information in the form of articles, checklists, tips, forums, and so on, some of which were helpful reference sources for this book. While many of them are also commercial ventures, this list excludes sites that are primarily or exclusively related to selling wedding-related products, without offering significant information.

AllWeddingCompanies.com *Description*: "Your planning guide offering great ideas and local resources for weddings! We are dedicated to categorizing local wedding vendors and their services and products."

BlackBride.com *Description*: "The place for black couples to plan their wedding."

blissezine.com *Site name*: "Bliss! Weddings—The Weddings Magazine." *Description*: "By creating a highly-interactive and user-friendly platform, the success . . . would rest greatly on the genuine and first-hand experiences of all those who contributed."

BridalTips.com *Slogan*: "Other sites give you the fluff, we give you the stuff!" *Description*: "Wedding Planning Tips and Avoiding Scams."

BrideOnline.com.au *Slogan*: "Australia's leading wedding directory."

Brides.com *Slogan*: "The Web site for the #1 bridal magazine."

BrideStuff.com *Slogan*: "You have the dream. We have the stuff." *Description*: "Created for the bride that is short on time or is not interested in shopping in the traditional brick-and-mortar retail stores."

bwedd.com *Site name*: "Brilliant Wedding Pages." *Description*: "Personal wedding Web sites and wedding ideas for the modern bride."

ConsciousWeddings.com *Description:* "We need to be willing to face our fears, honor our losses, and talk about more than napkin colors and flower arrangements as the big day nears."

confetti.co.uk *Slogan*: "The UK's no.1 site for weddings and special occasions."

CountryWeddings.com *Slogan*: "Wedding Guide and Honeymoon Planner." *Description*: "Our goal at Country Weddings is to help you enjoy planning your wedding and honeymoon celebration and location(s)."

Elegantbride.com *Slogan*: "The BEST of everything for the sophisticate bride." Web site of *Elegant Bride* magazine.

ForeverWed.com *Description*: "Christian Bridal and Wedding Guide."

freeweddingsites.com *Description*: "Are you interested in Wedding Freebies, Free Wedding Clip Art, Free Wedding Songs, and Free Services for Brides and Grooms? If so, you've come to the right place."

Frugalbride.com *Slogan*: "Canada's first frugal bridal Web site."

GettingRemarried.com *Description*: "THE comprehensive second wedding planning guide."

Handfasting.info *Description*: "Welcome lovers, and others who are seeking information about the rite of handfasting, a modern (usually) Pagan wedding ritual."

hitched.co.uk *Description*: "We aim to help you with every aspect of getting married from the engagement through to your honeymoon."

i-do.com.au *Description*: "Australia's No.1 Wedding Web site."

indiebride.com *Slogan*: "A site for the independent-minded bride." *Description*: "The words 'fantasy,' 'Cinderella' and 'princess' are strictly banned from our pages."

marriage.about.com *Description*: "Your guide to marriage."

MarriageRomance.com *Description*: "This site encourages married couples to write love letters and poems to each other and allows couples to submit marriage love stories, marriage advice, romance ideas, marriage humor, marriage prayers, and prayer requests."

ModernBride.com Web site of *Modern Bride* magazine.

Muslimwedding.org *Site name*: "1st Place Muslim Matrimonials." *Description*: "A unique place for marriage-minded Muslims around the world."

OurMarriage.com Includes sections on Planning, Community Forum, Wedding Etiquette, Unique Wedding Ideas, Customs and Traditions, Honeymoon Checklist, Local Wedding Vendors, and Let's Go Shopping!

OurWedding.com Leads to WeddingChannel.com (see below).

planyourwedding.net *Slogan*: "Your Definitive Resource For Wedding Planning in the United States."

Romance-Your-Wife.com *Slogan*: "'Growing' Love for a Lifetime." *Description*: "Where you will find a seemingly endless assortment of romantic ideas to romance your wife, plus FREE romance tips."

Take2Weddings.com *Description*: "If it's your second (or third . . .) wedding, this site is especially for you, but you'll also find it useful if you're looking for something really different."

TheKnot.com *Slogan*: "Everything you need for weddings. Wedding dresses to wedding cakes. Engagement rings, wedding favors, wedding gifts . . . we have it all!" *Description*: "The most comprehensive resource for couples seeking information and services to help plan their weddings and their future lives together."

Todays-Weddings.com *Site name:* Today's Weddings. *Slogan:* "Planning information for the busy bride of today."

ultimatewedding.com *Slogan:* "The Ultimate Internet Wedding Guide."

USABride.com *Description:* "Wedding, Wedding Dress, Wedding Favors, and Wedding Ideas."

usmarriagelaws.com *Description:* "Comprehensive guide to laws related to marriage in the United States and abroad."

Vibride.com *Description:* "The #1 online ethnic wedding destination, easy-to-use tools, and convenient, comprehensive gift registry."

VirtuallyMarried.com *Slogan:* "Create Your Own Wedding Web site. It's as easy as filling in a form."

WedAlert.com *Slogan:* "Your Wedding Planning Just Got Easier." *Description:* "Our mission is to match the local bride and groom with local wedding professionals."

WeddingBells.com *Slogan:* "Inspiring the celebration of marriage." Online edition of *WEDDINGBELLS*, a magazine published by Wedding-Channel.com (see below).

WeddingChannel.com *Slogan:* "Everything you need to plan the perfect wedding. Yours." *Description:* "We have all the ideas, advice, and information you need to plan your special day."

WeddingDetails.com *Slogan:* "Your complete wedding planning source." *Description:* "We have the most complete panel of experts to assist you in everything."

weddinggazette.com *Description:* "An underdog wedding monster—we now offer boatloads of info on how to plan out your budget, how to keep from killing certain family members, exhaustive theme ideas, plus tons of resources."

WeddingGuideUK.com *Description:* "The UK's first wedding Web site. You'll find in-depth articles, exciting features, and our award-winning discussion forums where you can meet and chat to other brides (and grooms) about your wedding 24 hours a day."

WeddingMagazine.com *Slogan:* "Your Online Wedding Guide." *Description:* "The online edition of *WEDDINGS* Magazine."

WeddingPlanningHints.com Features simple checklists and guidelines on Calendar, Location, Venue, Catering, Photography, Clothing, Rings, and Invitations.

WeddingPlanningLinks.com *Description:* "The Top Wedding Planning

Links and Hot Wedding Web Sites to help brides and grooms plan weddings."

weddings.about.com *Description*: "Your guide to weddings."

weddings.co.uk Includes United Kingdom–based information, announcements, articles, discussion forums, and products and services.

WeddingsAtWork.com *Slogan*: "We put the WOW! in your wedding!" *Description*: "An Internet-based resource center on Philippine/Filipino weddings."

WeddingSolutions.com *Slogan*: "For All Your Wedding Needs." *Features*: My Wedding, Fashion and Beauty, Local Vendors, Reception Sites, Honeymoon Sites, Shopping, Registry, Wedding Stories.

weddingspastandpresent.co.uk *Description*: "This is a wedding site with a difference, where you are invited to share memories of your wedding day."

WeddingUSA.com *Slogan*: "Planning Your Wedding . . . Is Now Easier." *Description*: "WeddingUSA features bridal stories, wedding planning guides, marriage requirements, a message board, and more."

Weddingzone.net *Slogan*: "The Ultimate Wedding and Party Planning Guide." *Description*: "This cool nationwide webzine and directory of wedding and party services will help you find everything you need to make your wedding ceremony and wedding reception an unforgettable affair!!!"

wednet.com *Slogan*: The Internet's Premier Wedding Planning Site." *Description*: "We're here to help you plan the biggest day of your life."

wedthemes.com *Site name*: "Wedding Themes and More." *Description*: "Designed to help you create a wonderful and personalized theme wedding."

WhichWedding.co.uk *Slogan*: "Weddings without the leg-work . . . find everything you need online." *Description*: "A one-stop guide for all weddings, not just the obvious ones."

world-weddings.net *Slogan*: "Destination Weddings in Locations Abroad." *Description*: "Plans and manages bridal ceremonies and wedding receptions in several different romantic locations for weddings abroad."

world-wedding-traditions.net *Subtitle*: "Wedding Traditions and Customs around the World."

YouMarriedHim.com *Slogan*: "Where love is reborn and marriages thrive!" *Description*: "An integrated community of women who are either involved in a serious relationship, getting married, have just been married, or who have been married for many years. . . . We welcome you into our community to share with us in your laughter, tears, gripes, groans, and whatever else you would like to shell out."

WEDDING AND MARRIAGE BOOKS—IN THEIR OWN WORDS

▼▼

Books on weddings and marriage abound. Here are a few classics, along with a few delightful oddities, some of which were useful reference resources for this book.

Anastasio, Janet, Michelle Bevilacqua, and Stephanie Peters. *The Everything Wedding Book: Absolutely Everything You Need to Know to Survive Your Wedding Day and Actually Even Enjoy It!* Holbrook, MA: Adams Media, 2000. "Along with helping you plan out each aspect of your wedding, . . . also explains how to alleviate a lot of the pressure and many of the hassles."

Baldridge, Letitia. *Legendary Brides: From the Most Romantic Weddings Ever, Inspired Ideas for Today's Brides.* Toronto/New York: Madison Press/HarperCollins, 2000. "'Borrows' unique touches from a century of memorable weddings and reinterprets them eloquently for a new generation of brides."

Barrett, Ann, and Wendy Moro. *The Funny Bride Guide: A Very Humorous, But Practical Guide for the Bride.* South San Francisco: Barmor Books, 1999. "Included: A special section on gift receiving! . . . Show sincere appreciation for the crocheted toilet paper cover, pioneer cookbook, or velvet replica of the Last Supper."

Blum, Marcy, and Laura Fisher Kaiser. *Weddings for Dummies.* New York: Hungry Minds, 1997. "Filled with expert advice from New York's premier wedding consultant, this unique guide unveils everything you need to make your wedding day a success."

Brady, Lois Smith. *Vows: Weddings of the Nineties from the New York Times.* New York: William Morrow, 1997. "Celebrates the oldest institution with great joy in this unique combination of luscious photography and lively profiles."

Bride's Magazine, editors of. *Bride's Book of Etiquette (Revised Edition).* New York: Perigee, 2003. "Offers the most up-to-date information on engagement and wedding planning, and realistic solutions for any problem that couples may encounter."

Cowie, Colin. *Weddings.* Boston: Little, Brown, 1998. "The man to whom celebrities such as Don Henley, Lisa Kudrow, Kelsey Grammer, Paula Abdul, and Kenny G turn for an unforgettable wedding . . . offers the modern bride-to-be an alternative approach to wedding design—one that is uniquely yours to fit your personality, taste, and style from start to finish."

Fields, Denise, and Alan Fields. *Bridal Bargains: Secrets to Throwing a Fantastic Wedding on a Realistic Budget.* Boulder, CO: Windsor Peak Press, 2002. "You need real-life solutions and creative ideas to plan a wedding without going bankrupt. . . . If Bridal Bargains doesn't save you $500 on your wedding, then we will give you a complete refund on the price of the book."

Fleming, Sue. *Buff Brides: The Complete Guide to Getting in Shape and Looking Great on Your Wedding Day.* New York: Villard Books, 2002. "A comprehensive, fully illustrated fitness book by a New York City personal trainer who has helped hundreds of brides get into shape over the past decade."

Gibson, Clare. *The Wedding Dress.* Philadelphia: Courage Books, and London: PRC Publishing, 2001. "This jewel of a book gives a captivating insight into both the bridal fashions and romantic values of previous generations."

Gottman, John M., Ph.D., and Nan Silver. *The Seven Principles of Making Marriage Work: A Practical Guide from the Country's Foremost Relationship Expert.* New York: Three Rivers Press, 1999. "Packed with practical questionnaires and exercises, . . . the definitive guide for anyone who wants their relationship to attain its highest potential."

Hunt, Mary. *Debt-Proof Your Marriage: How to Achieve Financial Harmony.* Grand Rapids, MI: Fleming H. Revell, 2003. "Covers everything you need for managing your money in harmony."

Ingram, Leah. *The Portable Wedding Consultant.* Chicago: Contemporary Books, 1998. "Offers brides-to-be thousands of expert tips and inside advice on every aspect of the wedding, from choosing attendants to finding help on-line."

Jones, Leslie. *Happy Is the Bride the Sun Shines On.* Chicago: Contemporary Books, 1995. "Reveals a world of wedding customs and beliefs that are sure to bring you a smile, a laugh, and maybe some luck on your special day."

Keller, Marisa, and Mike Mashon. *TV Weddings: An Illustrated Guide to Prime-Time Nuptials.* New York: TV Books, 1999. "A pictorial history of prime-time television weddings, with photographs, plots, and date, show, and character specifics of more than forty TV weddings from the 1950s to the present day."

Mack, Vicki. *The Groom's Guide.* Palos Verdes Estates, CA: Pinale Press, 2002. "Almost everything a man needs to know. A great reference for all the wedding details."

Matlins, Stuart M., editor. *The Perfect Stranger's Guide to Wedding Ceremonies.* Woodstock, VT: Skylight Paths, 2000. "There's no need to enter an unfamiliar atmosphere unprepared . . . telling you everything you need to know to avoid embarrassment, relax, and have a good time."

McBride-Mellinger, Maria. *The Perfect Wedding.* New York: Harper-Collins, 1997. "Welcome to the world of a thousand questions. . . . A comprehensive, knowledgeable text, illustrated throughout with beautiful color photographs, offers advice and creative ideas every step of the way."

Nettleton, Pamela Hill. *Getting Married When It's Not Your First Time.* New York: Quill, 2001. "Features a wealth of inspiring suggestions for handling delicate etiquette issues and navigating complex family ties."

Omelianuk, Scott, and Ted Allen. *Esquire's Things a Man Should Know about Marriage: A Groom's Guide to the Wedding and Beyond.* New York: Riverhead Books, 2000. "It's all right to be nervous. . . . It's all right to wonder, however fleetingly, whether you're making a terrible mistake."

Paul, Sheryl. *The Conscious Bride: Women Unveil Their True Feelings about Getting Hitched.* Oakland: New Harbinger, 2000. "Bridal counselor Sheryl Paul interviewed a diverse group of women who share their true feelings about the many concerns that can make an engagement a roller coaster of emotional ups and downs. Along with practical advice and support, you will find welcome acknowledgment of shared doubts and fears that so often run amok as wedding bells take their toll."

Post, Peggy. *Emily Post's Wedding Etiquette: Cherished Traditions and Contemporary Ideas for a Joyous Celebration.* New York: HarperResource, 2001. "With this book in hand, a couple can confidently blend the best of classic tradition with contemporary style, making this wondrous event a celebration to be remembered and treasured by all."

Post, Peggy. *Emily Post's Wedding Planner, 3rd Edition.* New York: Harper-Resource, 1999. "Leads you step-by-step through the practical details of planning your wedding, from announcing your engagement, to creating a realistic budget, to sending out thank-you notes."

Robbins, Li. *Going Bridal: How to Get Married Without Losing Your Mind.* New York: McGraw-Hill, 2003. "A wise and witty look at the emotional overload that surrounds wedding planning and suggests healthy ways to get from Yes! to I do!"

Roderick, Kyle, editor. *Married in the Movies.* San Francisco: Collins Publishers, 1994. "This delightful black and white collection captures some of the most famous matrimonial moments on the silver screen."

Roney, Carley. *The Knot Book of Wedding Flowers.* San Francisco: Chronicle Books, 2002. "From the ceremony arrangements to the posies for the bridesmaids, this comprehensive resource guides the happy couple through every aspect of floral decoration."

Shaw, Scott, and Lynn Beahan. *Let's Elope: The Definitive Guide to Eloping, Destination Weddings, and Other Creative Wedding Options.* New York: Bantam, 2001. "How to have the wedding your mother never dreamed of. . . . Filled with creative ideas for exchanging your vows in a memorable, personalized way that won't necessarily cost you a fortune—or your sanity."

Stewart, Arlene Hamilton. *A Bride's Book of Wedding Traditions: A Treasury of Ideas for Making Your Wedding the Most Memorable Day Ever.* New York: Hearst Books, 1995. "Helps today's bride fill her wedding with special meaningful touches by revealing traditions and customs that span cultures and centuries and have symbolized love, luck, fruitfulness, and joy from time immemorial."

Stewart, Martha. *The Best of Martha Stewart Living Weddings.* New York: Clarkson N. Potter, 1999. "In this breathtakingly beautiful volume, brides-to-be—or anyone participating in planning this joyous event—will find ideas and inspiration for every element of a wedding, including decorations, flowers, cakes, food, favors, and photography."

Thomashauer, Regina. *Mama Gena's Marriage Manual: Stop Being a Good Wife, Start Being a Sister Goddess.* New York: Simon and Schuster, 2004. "Throw out your preconceived notions of what marriage should be and allow yourself to construct a marriage based on your own personal gratification."

van Dijk, Peter. *The Clueless Groom's Guide: More Than Any Man Should Ever Know about Getting Married.* New York: McGraw-Hill, 2003. "Offers lighthearted commiseration, guidance, and a distinctly male take on the entire process of planning a traditional wedding. It gives you a sorely needed chuckle and some surprisingly useful advice."

Wallerstein, Judith S., and Sandra Blakeslee. *The Good Marriage: How and Why Love Lasts.* Boston/New York: Houghton Mifflin, 1995. "Based on a groundbreaking study of fifty couples who consider themselves happily married, . . . identifies the natural stages of a marriage and explains the nine psychological tasks . . . that must be undertaken by anyone committed to having a good marriage."

Wang, Vera. *Vera Wang on Weddings.* New York: HarperResource, 2001. "The world's most successful bridal gown designer shares her vision for this most important event . . . culled from years of experience in the wedding business."

INDEX

♥♥♥